THE
ARCHIVE
OF
MAGIC

THE FILM
WIZARDRY OF

FANTASTIC BEASTS
THE CRIMES OF
GRINDELWALD

INCANTÉ   CONJURÉ

ENVOUTÉ

THE ARCHIVE OF MAGIC

THE FILM WIZARDRY OF

FANTASTIC BEASTS
THE CRIMES OF GRINDELWALD

WRITTEN BY

Signe Bergstrom

DESIGNED BY

MinaLima

HARPER DESIGN
An Imprint of HarperCollins Publishers

WIZARDING WORLD

I've long been an admirer of J.K. Rowling's work. Before I ever imagined I would play Dumbledore, I read the Harry Potter series to my young children and was a fan of the film *Fantastic Beasts and Where to Find Them*. When I signed on to *Fantastic Beasts: The Crimes of Grindelwald*, I was thrilled to see the themes already present in J.K. Rowling's earlier work. One could say that the seeds planted in the first film found their roots in the second. Again and again, the characters—and, indeed, the audience itself—grapple with timeless questions: Who are we—and who do we want to be—in the face of evil? Will we stand together, despite our differences, to fight for the good of all humankind—wizards, witches, and the non-magical? And, lest we forget the beasts, J.K. Rowling has conjured a menagerie of creatures so fantastical that we're forced to reconcile their sense of wildness with our own. If we cannot protect the innocent, who can we save? It's powerful storytelling at its finest.

J.K. Rowling's characters wrest with universal notions—good versus evil; alliance versus the individual; us versus them—and usually emerge stronger and more compassionate for it (villains excepted, of course). For an actor, it's a gift for a writer to be so intimately aware of your character, to know his or her background, and to have an idea about how he or she came to be. In my case, J.K. Rowling's understanding of Dumbledore was paramount to mine. Being a reader of Harry Potter, I was, of course, familiar with Dumbledore, but I didn't have an inkling of who he was as a young man. Fortunately, I was lucky enough to spend an afternoon with J.K. Rowling, and she generously shaded in the details of his younger years—who he was before he became the headmaster audiences know and love. She also gave me insight into how he becomes the wizard we all come to know in Harry Potter.

The Crimes of Grindelwald, however, doesn't revolve solely around any one character; it's much larger than that. For as much as J.K. Rowling understands Dumbledore and his journey, she knows everyone else's, too, and what makes them tick—from Newt's inner struggles and Tina's quiet pride to the emotional intricacies of Jacob and Queenie to the manipulative charm of Grindelwald, down to Pickett the Bowtruckle. While everyone is on his or her own individual journey, several cross paths. Indeed, some, whether knowingly or not, are set on a

crash course with one another. The story itself is but a sum of their collective parts.

Nowhere is this concept more applicable than on a film set. Actors and actresses are but one unit of talent among countless other teams of extraordinary individuals whose skills range from the artistic to the technical, and everything in between. Filmmaking, especially on a movie with such a wide array of design, set, costuming, and technical elements, requires artistic collaboration of the highest degree. It's especially lovely when the collaborative process comes together in such a fluid, easy way. I've been fortunate enough to make films for years, but there's something very special about this one. Director David Yates created an on-set environment that fostered a sense of camaraderie: Everyone was genuinely excited to show up to work, put in the hard hours, and breathe life into his cinematic vision.

Fantastic Beasts: The Crimes of Grindelwald is a deeply imaginative film, and I believe that imagination, whether on page or on screen, has the power to heal and transform lives. It can inspire hope and spread goodwill. Indeed, if there's one thing I've learned from playing Dumbledore, it's that compassion is greater than any one spell. In the end, we don't need magic to stand together for what's right (though it certainly helps).

—Jude Law, 2018

Dumbledore (Jude Law) speaks with Leta Lestrange (Zoë Kravitz) at Hogwarts School of Witchcraft and Wizardry.

FILMMAKING ALCHEMY

"Sometimes you think the bigger the project, the less heart that goes into it. But with this film, that hasn't been the case at all. There's so much heart and so much care." —ACTRESS ZOË KRAVITZ

When *Harry Potter and the Deathly Hallows*, the final novel in J.K. Rowling's bestselling series, was published in July 2007 and part two of the accompanying final film was released four years later, a collective hush fell over fans, cast, and crew of the Wizarding World. Producer David Heyman says, "When Harry Potter finished with the eighth film, there was a combination of excitement and sadness. Excitement to have the time to embrace new projects . . . and sadness because it was a family who made those films, and it was such a great world to be a part of. So, when the opportunity arose to come back into the wonderful world that Jo Rowling had created, I leapt at it." That opportunity, of course, was 2016's *Fantastic Beasts and Where to Find Them*.

Camera operator Vince McGahon (left), director of photography Philippe Rousselot (middle), and director David Yates (right).

7

In the Harry Potter novels and films, the majority of the action, if not at Hogwarts, is rooted in Britain. In *Fantastic Beasts and Where to Find Them*, the lens widens to encompass New York City, and in *Fantastic Beasts: The Crimes of Grindelwald*, the second film of the five-part series, the lens opens further still as viewers are transported from the Big Apple to London—stopping off at some familiar stomping grounds, such as Hogwarts School of Witchcraft and Wizardry, along the way—to Paris, the City of Lights. Fantastically global, this expansion isn't relegated to matters of background. With *The Crimes of Grindelwald*, screenwriter J.K. Rowling introduces audiences to more characters (some of whom cross over to the Potter world), thrilling plotlines that span decades, and dazzling new spells. Newt Scamander's menagerie also multiplies: fan-favorite beasts, such as the Niffler and Pickett the Bowtruckle, usher in a bevy of new creatures.

In assembling the crew for *The Crimes of Grindelwald*, director David Yates and producer David Heyman didn't need to look far: a vast majority of the crew from the first film came back on board. Much of the talented crew—illustrators and

animators, graphic designers, tailors and cutters, set designers and builders, and countless other artisans and craftspeople—also worked on the Harry Potter films, which not only made the work flow faster and, in some instances, easier, but also helped to create a familial environment on set.

With everyone already knowing the ropes, creativity is given free rein. Systems are already in place, and key elements created for the other films—props, costumes, and graphic elements—are either repurposed or adopted whole. Having a nearly seamless transition between the two films doesn't mean anyone took a back seat, however. Heyman says, "We're questioning and challenging everything we did on the first film. We're kicking ourselves, saying, 'What can we do better? How can we improve the way this looks?' That way, we can apply all those lessons learned." Filmmaking is a bit like alchemy: it's the combination of lessons learned along with determination, grit, and grace that makes the hard work look like magic.

For *The Crimes of Grindelwald*, Yates strove to create a magical world so extraordinary that the magic itself is incidental. Heyman explains, saying, "Incidental magic is magic that's just accepted as a part of the environment and a part of the world, and you just throw it away." Because the magic is such an integrated component, it's commonplace.

Above: David Yates gives direction.
Right: Eddie Redmayne (Newt),
Dan Folger (Jacob), and William Nadylam
(Yusuf Kama).

It pops up everywhere and nowhere at the same time. Still, Yates tucks in surreally magical moments in the least expected places. At Circus Arcanus, for example, there was an idea that young children would blow bubbles so large that they could float around in them, telegraphing the message that magic exists everywhere. More important than the magic every witch and wizard possesses, however, is what she or he chooses to do with it—and sometimes it takes more than one individual to fight for what's right. Sometimes, it takes a menagerie of beasts and a fleet of wand-wielding witches and wizards (and a baker from New York City). David Heyman says, "The film is about so many things. It's about truths and half-truths, and it's about identity . . . It's a love story in so many ways. A thriller. It's comedic. It's emotional. It's about yearning and longing and love, and the inner struggle of all that stands in the way of that. It's emotionally potent and thrilling and . . . magical."

In other words, it's fantastic.

SHADES OF LIGHT AND DARK

"This is a different kind of morality tale." — SCREENWRITER AND PRODUCER J.K. ROWLING

The Crimes of Grindelwald mines the complicated humanity of each character as they balance the good of mankind against their own morality. The story traffics in shades of light and dark and explores those areas where individual and group beliefs overlap or conflict with one another. Ever the opportunist, Grindelwald rises to exploit those conflicts for personal advantage. Screenwriter and producer J.K. Rowling says, "This movie deals with the rise of an autocrat, or a man who will be an autocrat if he gets the chance . . . Grindelwald is a very seductive character and hopefully people will understand why even good-hearted characters are persuaded by him as he begins to gain power."

Rowling says, "David Yates and I have sat together and laughed about how this is not a straightforward story . . . You just can't reduce it to the good guys versus the bad guys because good guys cross over, bad guys are redeemed." While Grindelwald's appetite for complete dominion crosses over to dark, his intention — to bring the wizarding world out from the shadows — was rooted in a sense of idealism shared by none other than Dumbledore. Rowling says, "The relationship between Grindelwald and Dumbledore is key to making

Dumbledore. They met when they were very young, late teens, and they are both outstanding wizards . . . In this movie, you're just getting a taste of what their relationship is and what it will be." If their relationship informed much of Dumbledore's personality, its fissure set the stage for a battle of epic proportions — Dumbledore soon finds his ideals opposed to those of his former friend in *The Crimes of Grindelwald*.

For J.K. Rowling, the relationship between Grindelwald and Dumbledore was a unique opportunity to connect the worlds of Fantastic Beasts and Harry Potter. She says, "We meet ancestors and relatives of characters in the Beasts movies who are seen in the Potter books . . . At the same time, though, I'm telling a discrete story within the Fantastic Beasts franchise that is only hinted at in the Potter books, which is the rise of Grindelwald, who was a wizard who seriously threatened the security of the wizarding and the larger world, and his antagonist, Dumbledore, who of course is a key character in the Potter books. This was a backstory that I always had lots of ideas about, and now I get to tell it, which is artistically really satisfying."

THE WORLD
OF GRINDELWALD

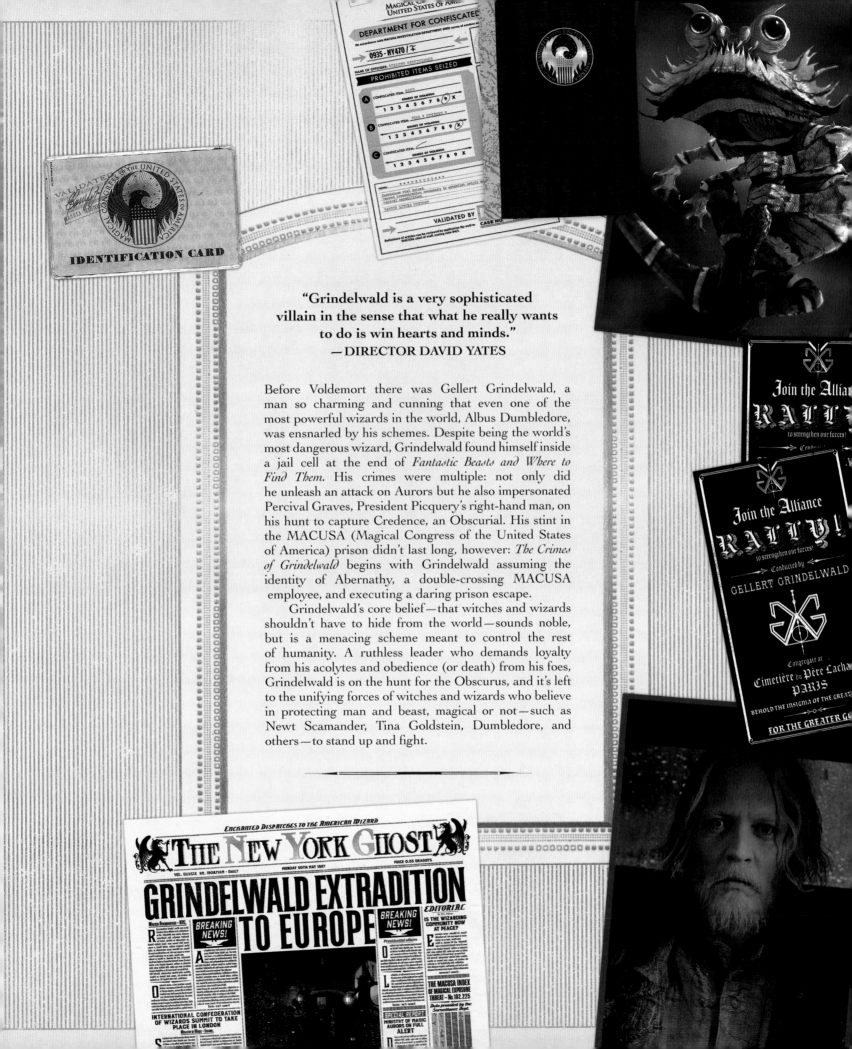

"Grindelwald is a very sophisticated
villain in the sense that what he really wants
to do is win hearts and minds."
—DIRECTOR DAVID YATES

Before Voldemort there was Gellert Grindelwald, a
man so charming and cunning that even one of the
most powerful wizards in the world, Albus Dumbledore,
was ensnarled by his schemes. Despite being the world's
most dangerous wizard, Grindelwald found himself inside
a jail cell at the end of *Fantastic Beasts and Where to
Find Them*. His crimes were multiple: not only did
he unleash an attack on Aurors but he also impersonated
Percival Graves, President Picquery's right-hand man, on
his hunt to capture Credence, an Obscurial. His stint in
the MACUSA (Magical Congress of the United States
of America) prison didn't last long, however: *The Crimes
of Grindelwald* begins with Grindelwald assuming the
identity of Abernathy, a double-crossing MACUSA
employee, and executing a daring prison escape.

Grindelwald's core belief—that witches and wizards
shouldn't have to hide from the world—sounds noble,
but is a menacing scheme meant to control the rest
of humanity. A ruthless leader who demands loyalty
from his acolytes and obedience (or death) from his foes,
Grindelwald is on the hunt for the Obscurus, and it's left
to the unifying forces of witches and wizards who believe
in protecting man and beast, magical or not—such as
Newt Scamander, Tina Goldstein, Dumbledore, and
others—to stand up and fight.

INTRODUCING
GELLERT GRINDELWALD

"A powerful wizard will get through most things." — PROP MAKER PIERRE BOHANNA

Grindelwald imprisoned at MACUSA.

Gellert Grindelwald, played by Johnny Depp, is a formidable and complex character known for his sinister charm and talent for rallying acolytes to his cause. The platinum-haired wizard and revolutionary believes in the triumph of magical blood. To his mind, he's working for the greater good: Witches and wizards shouldn't have to live a life of secrecy. Instead, they should emerge from the shadows as a dominating force to rule non-wizards and those born of lesser blood. His worldview ultimately leads to an epic confrontation between his followers and those on the side of freedom.

In the Harry Potter series, it was obvious that Voldemort, who killed numerous people and struck horror into the hearts of many more, was a villain. Grindelwald, however, is much more nuanced, and his power to manipulate and seduce is just as strong as any spell cast from a wand. Director David Yates says, "Grindelwald is a

Grindelwald's prop books and MACUSA documents for confiscated items.

VALIDATED BY:

CASE NO.
935-470

MAGICAL CONGRESS OF THE
UNITED STATES OF AMERICA

DEPARTMENT FOR CONFISCATED ITEMS

(In accordance with MACUSA INVESTIGATION DEPARTMENT (MID) terms of conduct and by law No. 3748/274.)

0935 - NY470 / ⊤

NAME OF OFFENDER: GELLERT GRINDELWALD

PROHIBITED ITEMS SEIZED

A CONFISCATED ITEM: WAND

GRADES OF VIOLATION

1 2 3 4 5 6 7 8 9 X

B CONFISCATED ITEM: VIAL · UNKNOWN

GRADES OF VIOLATION

1 2 3 4 5 6 7 8 9 X

C CONFISCATED ITEM:

GRADES OF VIOLATION

1 2 3 4 5 6 7 8 9 X

PLEASE REFER TO THE FOLLOWING LAWS.

NOTES: ***URGENT***

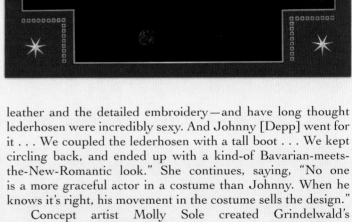

much more credible threat to all the values that are so important to those people who believe in love and light and understanding and curiosity. Grindelwald makes a case that's compelling because he pretends he's one of us. He pretends to empathize with us, and he does it in a very sophisticated way, which makes Grindelwald probably the most dangerous villain ever." Add to this the fact that even Albus Dumbledore cannot confront Grindelwald head-on, and it's clear this is a wizard with unfathomable powers of persuasion.

Grindelwald is the character everyone loves to hate. Actress Alison Sudol, who plays Queenie Goldstein, confesses that she

would have loved to play the part herself—if she weren't Queenie, that is. She says, "There's something so delicious about playing a villain . . . There's something very fun about being bad and really having a good time with it. He's a chameleon—one way with one person and then another to someone else and it's obviously an incredibly destructive, terrible characteristic to have as a human but quite fun to play as an actor." To help him step into the role, Depp worked with costume designer Colleen Atwood. They discussed the origins of Grindelwald's character and how Depp could best embody his qualities. The duo started with the character's name: Grindelwald suggested an alpine twist. Atwood says, "I've always loved Bavarian clothing—the punched

leather and the detailed embroidery—and have long thought lederhosen were incredibly sexy. And Johnny [Depp] went for it . . . We coupled the lederhosen with a tall boot . . . We kept circling back, and ended up with a kind-of Bavarian-meets-the-New-Romantic look." She continues, saying, "No one is a more graceful actor in a costume than Johnny. When he knows it's right, his movement in the costume sells the design."

Concept artist Molly Sole created Grindelwald's vial necklace. Sole says, "I tried to get my head around who Grindelwald was. What things were important to him? . . . He was obsessed with the Deathly Hallows." Sole used this obsession as her conceptual springboard and

Grindelwald stands behind a carriage that doubles as a hearse.

designed a piece of jewelry that references the Deathly Hallows, incorporating symbols for the Invisibility Cloak, the Elder Wand, and the Resurrection Stone into its design. (The triangle symbolizes the cloak; the line symbolizes the wand; and the circle represents the stone.) The result is a deeply personal artifact, something Sole feels Grindelwald himself could have made. Having these kinds of talismans helps to ground Grindelwald's character in reality. His physical attributes—the costume and the hair, and his two different-colored eyes— are but a slice of the character. The real magic is Depp's portrayal. Speaking about Grindelwald, William Nadylam, the actor who plays Yusuf Kama, says, "It's the charisma. You want to be his friend. You want to be with him. He looks like a winner."

GRINDELWALD'S WAND

In this film, audiences watch Grindelwald wield the Elder Wand. Throughout the course of wizarding history, the Elder Wand has changed hands several times; Grindelwald himself stole it from the wandmaker Gregorovitch. So named because it's made of elder wood, the wand is considered the world's most powerful. It has a length of fifteen inches and features a Thestral tail-hair core.

A BAD REPUTATION

"However ugly, however dangerous, his reputation is the worst—and the best." —J.K. ROWLING, script for *The Crimes of Grindelwald*

Grindelwald's name precedes his bad reputation: his rap sheet is long. While Newt Scamander and Tina Goldstein were able to apprehend Grindelwald at the end of *Fantastic Beasts and Where to Find Them* using the Swooping Evil as well as a one-two combo—the Summoning Charm and the Revelio Charm—it doesn't take long for Grindelwald to recruit MACUSA's Abernathy, who helps spring him from prison.

Grindelwald's daring jail break is a cinematic feat that brought all elements of cast and crew together. To create the rollicking spectacle, David Yates and Giles Asbury mocked up storyboards, which became the visual foundation for the effects team. Visual effects supervisor Christian Manz says, "We built out the sequence over five months, trying out different ideas. We've got a flying carriage. We've reintroduced broomsticks. Eunice Huthart, our stunt coordinator, has come up with a great rig for the brooms, which is different from what was done on the Harry Potter films . . . It's been a massive collaborative process."

To transport Grindelwald from MACUSA's basement prison cell to the Thestral carriage waiting atop the building's roof, the art department stripped the building's interior to make it an open, eerily windswept place—and created all the more space for the camera to move about freely. After Grindelwald is loaded into the carriage, the carriage quickly plummets: in order for the Thestrals—the skeletal winged horses—to get through a gap in the attic, they have to tuck in their wings, which causes the sudden turbulence. It's one instance where the set design drives the action, and the art department, visual effects, and stunt team are in lockstep with one another.

While the story unfolds at a clipped pace, audiences are sure to notice the Elder Wand, held by both Abernathy and Grindelwald. These clues—the Elder Wand, the Thestral carriage, the broomsticks, and more—signal that not only is this film a fantastic one, it's also linked to the world of Harry Potter. As soon as the carriage bursts through the roof of MACUSA's headquarters, audiences know they're in for a ride, and with Grindelwald at the helm, it promises to be dark, dangerous, and thrilling.

Grindelwald, imprisoned in a MACUSA jail cell.

Grindelwald's skull hookah.

THE THESTRAL CARRIAGE

"It's almost like a roller-coaster ride."
—SPECIAL EFFECTS SUPERVISOR DAVID WATKINS, on the film's opening scene

Top and middle: Concept art for the Thestral carriage.
Bottom: A VFX rendering with an added background.

Following the record number of visual effects in *Fantastic Beasts and Where to Find Them*, this film boasts a few of its own, starting with the rollicking Thestral carriage ride.

Thestrals are skeleton-like, leather-winged horses. Despite their horselike bodies, they have a reptilian quality, too: their heads are dragonish in form, their pupilless eyes white. Visible only to those who have witnessed death, Thestrals are, by their very nature, eerie. Audiences familiar with the world of Harry Potter know that Hogwarts School of Witchcraft and Wizardry maintains a trained fleet of Thestrals, who transport students via carriage from Hogsmeade Station to the gates of the castle

and, in *Harry Potter and the Deathly Hallows—Part 1*, were used by the Order to help escort Harry from the Dursleys' home to the Burrow. Known for their speed, Thestrals are ideal substitutions for broomsticks.

For the Thestral carriage featured in *The Crimes of Grindelwald*, the art department commissioned three full-size carriages. The team also built several different interiors for the carriages, including one that could safely be filmed when filled with water. The main carriage was hoisted onto several gimbals (pivoted supports for rotating the cameras) and rigs. Visual effects supervisor Christian Manz says, "We've got rigs to drive them to make it look as if they're really flying around." Previously, the crew had used remote-controlled and computer-controlled cameras. With the rig setup, however, the team could shoot the sequence for themselves. Manz says, "We might be able to get broom riders in with the carriage next to each other and them shooting across from one to the other," rather than adding them to the scene during postproduction, for example. Manz continues, saying, "Hopefully, it'll make the scene feel like it's a real pursuit."

The camera rigs themselves are plentiful. Special effects supervisor David Watkins says, "We've added a couple of additional rigs to the underside of the carriage that Grindelwald's holding on to. There are different configurations of the carriage or different parts of it mounted in different ways for certain shots." The special effects team largely depends

Johnny Depp filming the Thestral carriage sequence.

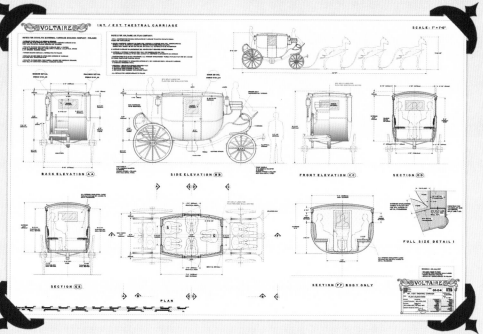

The cast and crew work with green screens and CGI to create the rollicking visual effects of Grindelwald's daring escape.

on rigs, gimbals, and waldos to help design shots. Watkins explains the magic of the waldo, saying, "When we're designing the shots with the gimbal, we have a waldo, or mimicking model, on our desk, back at the control system. And whatever we do with our model is transferred to the gimbal that's on set. A lot of the shots were designed live and then we would record a move until we got what we were after. The waldos are invaluable in our world." The waldos give the team freedom to play around and work live—invaluable when it comes to filming a scene that necessitates both coordinated choreography among the cameras and a sense of reckless, fast-paced pursuit. Working closely together, the cast and crew were able to elicit the heart-pounding excitement of an out-of-control jailbreak with precision and control.

THE EVOLUTION OF BROOMSTICK DESIGN

In *The Crimes of Grindelwald*, broomsticks are seen on-screen but for a few seconds and, more than anything, serve as background dressing. Yet the care and thought that went into their creation speaks volumes about how every prop is important and artisanship is king. Concept artist Molly Sole says, "You have to look at what was done before so that you've got an idea of the actual evolution of the broomstick design . . . Is the broomstick design simpler [than from those in the

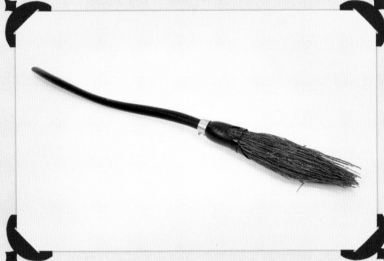

Harry Potter films] because it's an earlier time period? Do the French do things differently?" Chasing down answers to these questions and others yielded broomsticks that replicate the elegance of the art nouveau style that informs much of the set design. For those broomsticks used in the opening chase

sequence, however, elegance wasn't a priority; speed was. Streamlined and wickedly beautiful, the broomsticks are made to look *fast*.

While it's important that each broomstick match the stunt team's requirements for flight, the art department also has more real-world, practical concerns. Sole says, "There are certain sizes and certain shapes needed by the stunt guys. [Head prop maker] Pierre Bohanna will liaise with the stunt guys and find out their rig requirements." The shape of the rig can affect the brooms' overall design. In previous films, the stunt person rode the broom, which was on a gimbal or on a rig. In this film, however, the rig is attached to the rider, which allows them to do more authentic movements. Design-wise, it means the brooms no longer need stirrups.

Above: French broomstick props. Right: Concept art for a Quidditch broomstick.

GRINDELWALD'S ACOLYTES

"David [Yates] was keen to avoid a homogenized sense of blank-palette baddies." —ACTOR KEVIN GUTHRIE

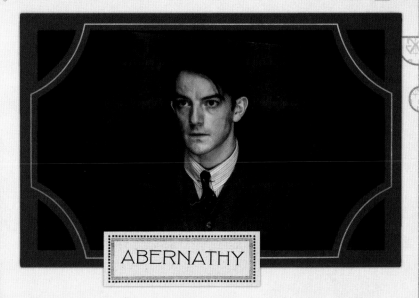

ABERNATHY

ROSIER

Grindelwald's acolytes are fully realized characters, each with specific eccentricities and personalities. Actor Kevin Guthrie, who plays Abernathy, says, "We, the actors, were selected in our own weird and wonderful ways, and bring an individuality to each of our characters." Audiences already know Abernathy, Grindelwald's right-hand man. In the first Fantastic Beasts film, he was straitlaced and strict, an American wizard and model official of MACUSA, and supervisor to Tina and Queenie Goldstein. In the second film, he becomes a double agent, a disciple of sinister proportion. Guthrie says, "He's fresh meat on the tour; he's the whipping boy . . . Abernathy is desperate to please, desperate for some sort of assessment of positivity from Grindelwald." Abernathy's transformation wouldn't be complete without a change of costume. Costume designer Colleen Atwood outfitted Abernathy in clothing that communicates a sense of daring and risk taking; gone is the bookish look of a man focused on his profession and in its place is a streamlined-yet-seductive look. More important than his clothing, however, is his ability to carry out Grindelwald's orders with precision. "In terms of his ability to deliver and execute a spell," says Guthrie, "he's simple and to the point. There's nothing wishy-washy or flashy."

Besides Abernathy, Grindelwald has recruited a host of other henchmen/acolytes, including Nagel, played by Claudius Peters;

MacDuff, played by Andrew Turner; Krafft, played by Simon Meacock; Krall, played by David Sakurai; Carrow, played by Maja Bloom; and Vinda Rosier, played by Poppy Corby-Tuech. (Rosier is also the last name of a Death Eater in the Harry Potter books and Carrow is the same surname of Amycus and Alecto, two Death Eaters who appear in the Harry Potter films.)

To help distinguish each acolyte, Atwood added plenty of personalized detail to their largely tonally red-and-green "uniforms": Rosier, Grindelwald's second-in-command, dons a pointy witch hat; MacDuff is outfitted with a chain decorated with everything from a rabbit's foot to a collection of human teeth; Krafft is beset in a militaristic-looking jacket. The other acolytes are dressed as different-styled heavies. Some wear triple-belted straps over jackets, paired with sharp-edged hats complete with pointer feathers, a conscious nod to fashions favored by European fascists during the 1930s.

This distinct group of wizards don't see themselves as being on the wrong side of history, which makes them all the more real . . . and dangerous. They consider themselves revolutionaries. Claudius Peters, who plays Nagel, says, "They want to make the world a better place, from their point of view anyway, and they're part of Grindelwald's team in order to do that."

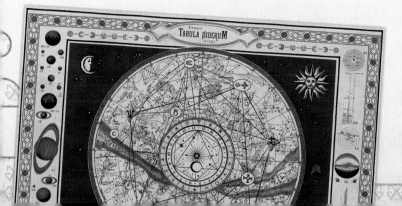

KRALL

CREDENCE BAREBONE

"He doesn't particularly care about survival except as a mechanism of discovery."
—ACTOR EZRA MILLER on his character, Credence

Ezra Miller, the actor who portrays Credence Barebone, says that "from the second we were done with the first film, I was extremely excited and determined to work on the continuation of Credence's arc." Miller was particularly enthusiastic because he's a fan of J.K. Rowling's work, citing her Potter series as a launchpad from which he explored his own burgeoning imagination. Miller says, "The idea of magic, which to me is the true unknown operative juice of every single thing . . . has been central to me my whole life. J.K. Rowling's work was a haven for those secret understandings to dwell in. It gave them a place to grow, to not be diminished in the world . . . Magic is real. Magic is everything . . . To then get to participate in filling out that world and following different trajectories of the imaginative mind . . . it continues to be one of the great honors and privileges of my life."

Credence embarks on a journey of self-discovery, having cast off the chains of the abuse and repression that he suffered at the hands of his adoptive mother, Mary Lou Barebone.

Credence and the Maledictus outside a Parisian apartment.

DANGER

Miller says, "Much of wh...
knows now to be a lie ... ...
to intentionally control th...
energy Credence has insi...
man. In a sense, Credence...
victim to being a survivo...
sense of responsibility a...
inner magic has the powe...
elaborates, saying, "He's...
inherent power ... He's...
that at this point in a wiza...
so he's running out of tim...

In the wreckage of ...
Philanthropic Society chu...
and sets off to Europe in...
gets entangled along the...
Skender, ringmaster to ...
he's, once again, put him...
"is just another cage." Ur...
tracked by several wizard...
Grimmson and Tina Gol...
as an Auror. Credence ta...
the Maledictus, a woman...
transform into a snake.

Desperate for the ke...
holds all the answers: C...
of the young man's tru...
Miller says, "Grindelwa...
people who manipulate ...
part strategy: give somec...
enemy." For his part, Gr...
want anything from Cre...
by his all-consuming des...
for pondering the Dark v...

CREDENCE

Irma Dugard.
Paris, FRANCE.

e Barebone

Fabric swatches
and a sketch of
Credence's costume.

DEPT. INFORMATION SHEET

Supplier

MISAN

BERNSTEIN & BANLEY

WHALEYS

from stock

Width / Notes
Price per metre or yd
Qty & date bought

CAUTION
MAGICAL CREATURE

COSTUME DESIGN
COLLEEN ATWOOD

A member of the costume department inspecting and adjusting costumes.

"You feel the shadow of darkness. There's a fog. There's a lot of atmosphere in the film." — COSTUME DESIGNER COLLEEN ATWOOD

Costume designer Colleen Atwood has won four Academy Awards. Her most recent win was for her work on *Fantastic Beasts and Where to Find Them*. These awards, she says, only make her want to "up the game," and for the second film in the Fantastic Beasts franchise, she's done just that.

The film is set in 1927, and the costumes are period pieces with a twist. Atwood's amped up the standard tones of the time—browns and blacks and grays, though those are present, too—with tonally rich red hues and royal purples alongside deep blues and dark greens. The result is a sumptuously dressed ensemble that, amid the gritty streets, manages to look of the time—and slightly otherworldly, too. Atwood admits the clothing is "a little more forward than the actual time period . . . I pushed everything into a more glamorous kind of world." She elaborates, saying, "The skirts are a little bit long. The silhouettes are much more fitted. The men's clothes are slightly more tailored. The trousers are a little wider. There are subtle differences, but they make for more flow and movement. And then I've done more fantastical-looking hats."

Overall, the clothing is more glamorous than what was featured in *Fantastic Beasts and Where to Find Them* and, is slightly more sophisticated, too, imbued with a certain European sense of fashion and flair. The characters have grown up a bit since the first film, and it makes sense that their clothing would reflect a more mature sensibility. Atwood says, "They're in a different phase of their lives and mingling and coming into contact with a higher echelon of the wizarding world, which is a very sophisticated world set in Paris." To capture the look and feeling of Paris, Atwood studied the fashion of Versailles as well as the grittier side of the city, including its sexy, musical underworld of cabarets and follies.

Atwood begins the costume-design process with an idea of a shape she wants. "I'm not a person who particularly starts with a sketch," she says. Instead, she begins with photographic references and then sits down with the cutter. She says, "We look at a cutout shape—called the muslin on the form—and sometimes it's in the real fabric. Sometimes, it's just a cotton toile, and we draw on that, and we figure out where the different flow of the

Vinda Rosier

fabric is, and then we cut into the fabric, and sew it, and then we try it on the actor." Atwood works collaboratively with the actors, too, and engages them in conversation early on, asking them how they see their characters. Atwood says, "They can be specific about how they feel about a color, or the shape, the direction their costume is moving." Atwood strives to not only convey a sense of character with the clothing but also make sure everything fits properly, too. She says, "Ultimately, they're the people who have to live in the costume for months on end, so you want to make it comfortable for them."

To help organize her creative process, Atwood works cyclically, designing clothing for the different types of scene requirements or characters: wizards and witches (and anyone else deemed "magical") is one category; everyday clothing, another; clothing for over-the-top extravagant scenes, a third. Atwood says, "It's a gritty combination of a lot of different styles together," and each category has its attending distinctions. For the more magical characters, Atwood favored extreme silhouettes as a cinematic nod to the story's more film noir aspects. Grindelwald's acolytes—another category—don militaristic garb, albeit with a certain edge.

By no means is Atwood a one-woman show. A host of textile artists, cutters, sewers, dyers, and fitters work in the costume department. On any given day, a team of about one hundred and fifty people can have their hands full. (Her core team consists of around fifty or sixty people.) Turn around is tight: the department usually works about two weeks ahead of time but while one scene is being filmed, the team will simultaneously prep for the next one. Atwood jumps back and forth (from set to workshop and between scenes) as new costumes are established. Lead time before principal photography began was about four months, which, Atwood says, "is pretty fast for the scale of the show. A lot of the parts aren't cast initially, so you start with the people you know are in the film, and then as the rest of the cast comes together, you manufacture their costumes," and manufacturing doesn't stop once filming starts. Atwood's team works at a full-throttle pace to deliver incredible, hand-tailored, one-of-a-kind costumes that capture both the mood of the film and the individual quirks of each character.

HATS

Because hats were the fashion accessory in the 1920s, Atwood's team created everything from flat caps (practical, snap-brim caps common with the working class) to fedoras (considered the iconic man's hat of the period with a fairly high crown) to its female counterpart, the cloche, which comes down to cover most of a lady's hair. Atwood, however, pushed the fashion a bit into the early 1930s because hats were much more sculptural during those years, and sculptural freedom gave her the chance to be more daring in her design approach. Most of the extras wear the hats of the everyday workingman or workingwoman, but other performers are in a class of their own. The French Aurors are outfitted in the most magical of hats (next to the traditional witch's hat, of course): the beret.

LONDON

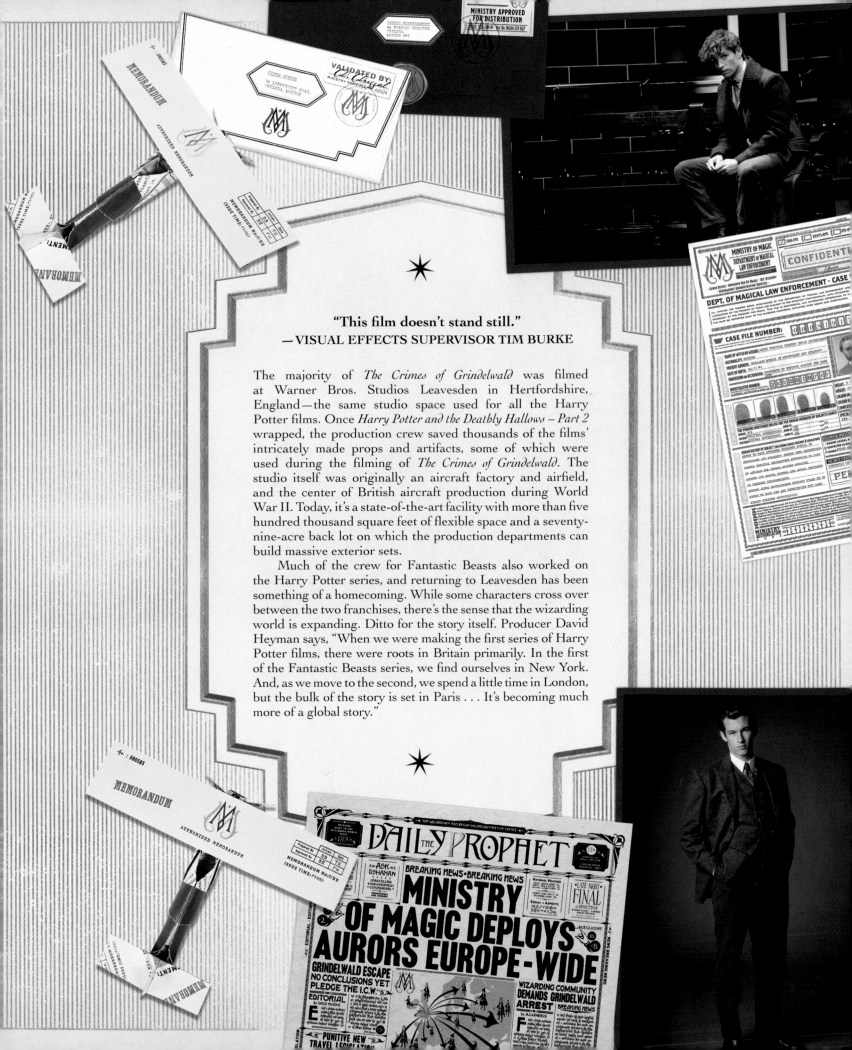

"This film doesn't stand still."
—VISUAL EFFECTS SUPERVISOR TIM BURKE

The majority of *The Crimes of Grindelwald* was filmed at Warner Bros. Studios Leavesden in Hertfordshire, England—the same studio space used for all the Harry Potter films. Once *Harry Potter and the Deathly Hallows – Part 2* wrapped, the production crew saved thousands of the films' intricately made props and artifacts, some of which were used during the filming of *The Crimes of Grindelwald*. The studio itself was originally an aircraft factory and airfield, and the center of British aircraft production during World War II. Today, it's a state-of-the-art facility with more than five hundred thousand square feet of flexible space and a seventy-nine-acre back lot on which the production departments can build massive exterior sets.

Much of the crew for Fantastic Beasts also worked on the Harry Potter series, and returning to Leavesden has been something of a homecoming. While some characters cross over between the two franchises, there's the sense that the wizarding world is expanding. Ditto for the story itself. Producer David Heyman says, "When we were making the first series of Harry Potter films, there were roots in Britain primarily. In the first of the Fantastic Beasts series, we find ourselves in New York. And, as we move to the second, we spend a little time in London, but the bulk of the story is set in Paris . . . It's becoming much more of a global story."

THE MINISTRY OF MAGIC

MINISTRY OF MAGIC

IDENTITY CARD

027424♓3

Due to Newt Scamander's past transgressions, the Ministry of Magic is keeping tabs on him and has denied his travel documentation. Despite his brother, Theseus, working for the organization as Head of the British Auror Office, Newt has maintained an uneasy alliance with the British Ministry of Magic. Not one to follow orders, especially when a beast is in danger, Newt wasn't exactly forthcoming for the reasons of his last international trip. The only way Newt's travel documents will be reinstated and the ban lifted is if he joins the Ministry and helps a team led by Torquil Travers (played by Derek Riddell), the Head of Magical Law Enforcement, to track down Credence. Newt, ever distrustful of Aurors, denies their request. In his place, they appoint a nefarious man by the name of Gunnar Grimmson, a beast hunter, to find the Obscurial.

ONFIDENTIAL

Torquil Travers (Derek Riddell),
Head of Magical Law Enforcement.

Newt Scamander (Eddie Redmayne),
as he is asked to help capture and
destroy the Obscurus.

Audiences already know the Ministry of Magic and its vast network of departments. Producer David Heyman says, "In Harry Potter, we had Hogwarts and the Ministry of Magic. Those were our two central magical places . . . In this second film, however, we get to see so many more magical environments." And places audiences already know, like the Ministry of Magic, are seen with a fresh eye. Changes in detail may be subtle but are present nonetheless. Take the Ministry of Magic's insignia, for example. Graphic designers Miraphora Mina and Eduardo Lima tweaked the image ever so slightly. Mina says, "The first thing we did was to redesign the insignia because the one that we saw in the Harry Potter films would have been too modern for this time period. We're assuming it's been redesigned as the years have gone by." The graphics team kept to the color purple to stay familiar to Harry Potter. Because the institution is so traditional, its branding is, too. But, because it's also a place of magic, the purple signifies a "shift," as Mina says, "into a magical environment."

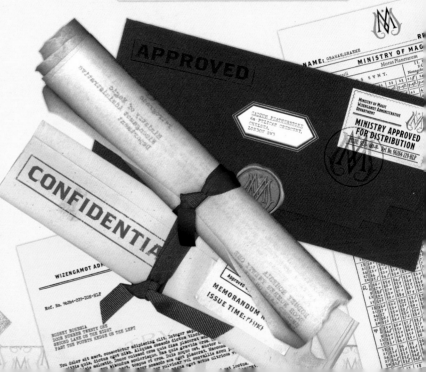

BUREAUCRATIC MAGIC

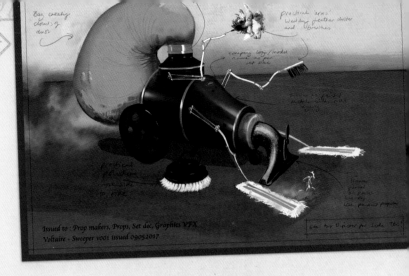

Despite being a bureaucratic entity, the Ministry of Magic still has some whimsical devices at its disposal, including everything from the dictograph and tickertape machines to the sweeper, a vacuum that looked positively futuristic for the early 1900s but is plenty old-school for today's audiences. Prop modeler Pierre Bohanna says, "We produced about one hundred tickertape machines for the film. Ribbony lengths of tickertape fly between the different departments, coming and going from these machines." But that's not all—a magical quill takes notes on the dictograph, which issues forth never-ending reams of parchment paper. Even at its most magical, the ministry depends on bureaucratic recording methods.

SWEEPER

The sweeper was originally designed by Adam Brockbank several years ago for the Harry Potter films, but was never built. For this film, the design team took Brockbank's initial idea and incorporated elements—even salvaged parts—from 1950s Hoover vacuums. While the machine isn't a period piece per se, it's still a throwback for modern-day audiences. During the design process, the team added a feather duster arm, dreamt up by Pierre Bohanna, that set decorator Anna Pinnock cleverly suggested should create as much dust as it cleans up.

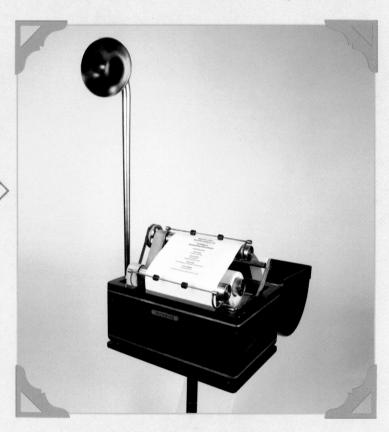

DICTOGRAPH

A majority of the on-screen props and objects are created by molding or casting, including the Ministry's dictograph. To create it, the modeling department worked off of a 3-D print. Supervising modeler Steve Wotherspoon explains, saying, "A drawing of an object or prop is done. Then, a pattern is made of the drawing. We transform the pattern into the hard object." Besides the dictograph—a telephonic instrument used for picking up and transmitting sound—the modeling department has replicated everything from marbles to heaps of French candies.

INTRODUCING
GUNNAR GRIMMSON

"Grimmson is Newt's nemesis." —ACTOR EDDIE REDMAYNE

GRIMMSON'S WAND

Worn-down and well-used, Grimmson's wand has seen a lot of action. Besides using it to hunt and track beasts, he also uses his wand, like other wizards, to cast spells. The Protego spell is especially helpful in that it conjures a shield, which comes in handy whenever Grimmson's being charged by a roaming beast (or a mal-intentioned witch or wizard).

Played by Ingvar Sigurðsson, Gunnar Grimmson is a sinister yet skilled beast hunter hired by the Ministry of Magic to track Credence. Hot on Credence's trail, Grimmson kills a character who holds a clue to the young man's identity, and, with nowhere else to seek help, Credence is left vulnerable to Grindelwald's nefarious machinations.

Grimmson is the dark twin of Newt: whereas Newt protects beasts and writes to teach the world about them, Grimmson tracks to kill. To his mind, the beasts pose a threat: their unpredictability could expose the wizarding world to non-wizards. Actor Eddie Redmayne says, "The two characters are polar opposites of one another, and their dynamic comes to full hilt." While audiences don't know the full story behind these two beast hunters, both are skilled at searching for beasts in remote parts of the world. Like Newt, Grimmson also has tools of the trade, albeit his instruments are designed to entrap and hunt rather than to heal.

Newt with Gunnar Grimmson
(Ingvar Sigurðsson).

INTRODUCING LETA LESTRANGE

"It was amazing to see the first film and know that I would get to play in that magical world."
—ACTRESS ZOË KRAVITZ

As a pure-blood witch from the powerful Lestrange family, Leta's name precedes her. Producer David Heyman says, "The Lestrange family name comes with a whole raft of expectations and associations, so Leta has to live with that. She also has a dark side. She's acted out and has done bad things in the past. But, that doesn't necessarily make her who she is. She's also someone who's decent . . . She has many wonderful qualities and she wrestles with what's expected of her and who she really is."

Zoë Kravitz was familiar with the Lestrange family via Helena Bonham Carter's performance as the sadistic witch Bellatrix Lestrange in the Potter series. (Fans may remember that Bellatrix was one of Voldemort's most dependable and dangerous subordinates.) Kravitz says, "I know where that family [the Lestranges] goes and what it means to them to be pure-blood . . . Leta was pitched to me as this woman who's kind of stuck in the middle . . . and isn't quite sure where she fits in in terms of being good or bad. I think she's somewhere in between. She's quite complicated, and I think we're all kind of like that, so it was an interesting path for me to develop."

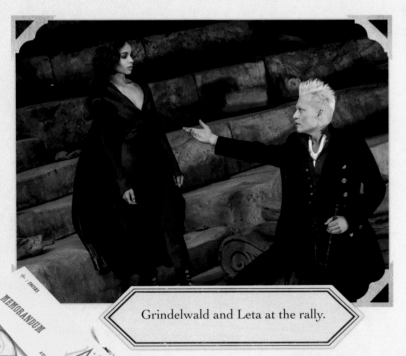

Grindelwald and Leta at the rally.

A tragic figure, Leta has secrets, which unravel throughout the course of the film. Audiences learn that her brother, Corvus, is mysteriously lost. Leta's lifelong sense of guilt, familial expectation, and pressure is immense. "Leta lives in a place emotionally where no one wants to be," says Kravitz. "She has a lot of guilt and self-loathing, and in order to play that role, I have to find that in myself . . . You have to go sit in those uncomfortable places where this woman, Leta, lives all the time. So even dipping in and out throughout the course of this film has been quite intense for me." Callum Turner, who plays Leta's fiancé and Newt's brother, Theseus, says, "Zoë brought a real depth to Leta . . . In a sense, she's sort of the heartbeat of the movie, and Zoë carries it off like it's nothing. It's amazing to watch." In Theseus, Leta finds a more than capable and confident partner, someone who's incredibly different from Newt, whom Leta had a close relationship with while both attended Hogwarts. Both Leta and Newt were outsiders, and that sensibility brought them together. Plus, as Kravitz says, "Newt sees this kind of beast, or as Leta would say, 'monster' in her and loves that about her and doesn't want to change a thing about her." Even though Leta's engaged to

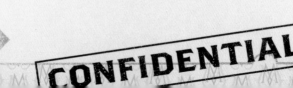

CONFIDENTIAL

Left: Leta, seated at a classroom desk at Hogwarts.

Theseus—a man who sees only the best in people, including his oddball brother—Newt still has a soft spot for her. In the first film, Queenie noticed a photo of Leta that Newt carried in his case and, using Legilimency to read his thoughts, asserted that Leta was a "taker" and not a "giver" in their relationship. Her comment, nonetheless, does not dissuade Newt's tenderness toward the girl he knew from Hogwarts.

Aware that her choices and actions may have significant consequences for her and her loved ones, Leta's internal struggle is deeply felt. Kravitz says, "I'm curious to see how people will receive her . . . I think David [Yates] is going to have a field day finding the balance between the lightness and the darkness," a task not unlike the one Kravitz undertook herself to portray the complicated witch.

Leta Lestrange

LETA LESTRANGE'S WAND

"We're not actually accessing magic, but sometimes it feels like we are because everyone is so committed to the story." —ACTRESS ZOË KRAVITZ

As an extension of the character, Leta's wand is both elegant and bold in appearance. Made of black ebony and featuring a raised silver detail on the handle, it's the perfect wand for a pure-blood aristocrat. Kravitz says, "My wand is appropriate for Leta," but, she admits, "I like Tina's wand . . . I like Newt's wand a lot. I have wand envy. But Leta's is very fancy."

INTRODUCING
THESEUS SCAMANDER

"It's been a real journey joining this film." —ACTOR CALLUM TURNER

When Callum Turner was a ten-year-old boy, he, like so many other children around the world, read *Harry Potter and the Sorcerer's Stone* (known as *Harry Potter and the Philosopher's Stone* in the UK), and went to bed dreaming he'd wake to find a letter of acceptance to Hogwarts, delivered by owl. He never got that letter but, twenty years later, he did get the call to play Theseus Scamander, Newt's older brother. The worlds collide . . .

As Head of the British Auror Office in the Ministry of Magic, Theseus is a part of the establishment in ways that his quirky brother, who was expelled from Hogwarts and became a Magizoologist, is not. Turner describes the differences between the brothers, saying, "He [Theseus] decided to fight the good fight [by joining the Ministry], whereas Newt is part of the rebellion." They're both on the same side, but fighting in very different ways. Other than that key detail, the brothers clearly care for one another. While Theseus may be a bit more self-assured and confident than Newt, they share a deep sense of humanity.

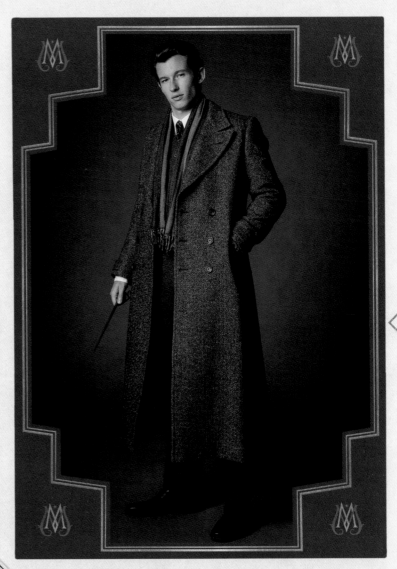

Theseus and Leta share a moment at Le Ministère des Affaires Magiques de la France.

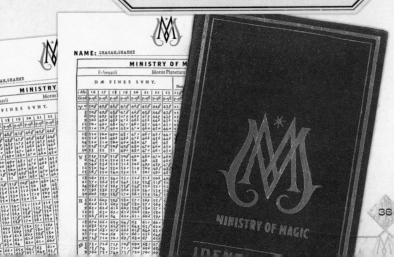

Not having any siblings himself, Turner found it a challenge to portray Newt's older brother, especially since he himself is younger than Eddie Redmayne. It helped that he and Redmayne were from the same town. Turner says, "Coincidentally, we both grew up in Chelsea . . . we grew up, a ten minutes' walk from each other . . . We both learned to swim in the same swimming pool, and things like that. We knew some of the same spots." By the time the actors began filming, they'd bonded and developed a sense of camaraderie no doubt shaped, in part, by their shared personal history. As his older brother, Theseus naturally looks out for Newt.

VALIDATED BY:

MINISTRY OFFICIAL   No. 48524

Turner didn't read the script until three weeks prior to filming. By the time he stepped into rehearsals, he had an idea of who Theseus was, but it still took some time for him to feel comfortable in the role. The costume—and wand—helped. Turner admits that he's stylistically very different from the character he portrays, joking, "I don't have that swagger." Besides its flashier touches, like the ankle swingers, Theseus's costume also telegraphs his fastidious nature. One look at his perfectly placed pocket squares and audiences know this is a meticulous—and fashionable—man.

Speaking about the filmmaking process itself, Turner says, "I think everyone on this—the producers, director, writer, actors, and the crew—is pulling in the same direction so there's no ownership over it, because ultimately it's not about you. You're a cog and the feeling is that everyone realizes that it's bigger than them . . . . Everyone has a valid or valuable place to be in, and it's just as important as the next person." Theseus could say the same about the Ministry and his family.

Newt and Theseus take cover.

Newt, Bunty, Leta, and Theseus at the book launch for *Fantastic Beasts and Where to Find Them.*

THESEUS SCAMANDER'S WAND

Theseus Scamander's wand is every bit as elegant and refined as Theseus is himself. Concept artist Molly Sole says, "It's made from tortoiseshell, a material that would be really rather elegant for a chap who's done well for himself. It matches his smart and snappy personality." Learning how to wield it with grace, however, was far from easy for Turner. "My relationship with my wand has been a volatile one," he admits. "I actually broke it on its first outing."

Theseus Scamander

CONFIDENTIAL

BUILDING A CITY

"These are fully working, functioning items and sets with real materials, real metal, real rivets. They last. You might see them for thirty seconds on-screen but they'll last for years and years to come." —SUPERVISING ART DIRECTOR MARTIN FOLEY

Newt and Dumbledore on the dome of St. Paul's Cathedral.

Concept art of Trafalgar Square, London.

Supervising art director Martin Foley says, "We would love to shoot on location." But on such a large-scale film, with scores of extras, complicated action scenes, and multi-layered special effects, it's nearly impossible to do so. He explains, saying, "To get authenticity you almost need to have control." By controlling the environment—literally building London from the ground up on studio sets—the team can generate their own version of London— or Paris or New York—and infuse the city's architecture with fantastical elements whenever necessary. The crew can also add on to existing sets, and create new environments as needed. Fans are already familiar with the interior of the Ministry of Magic; in this film, however, audiences see a new room, specially created for the scene of Newt's hearing.

With one hundred sets to do and about twenty-odd weeks to shoot them all, the crew moves at a clipped pace. The conceptual design

Dumbledore shares with Newt his concerns about Grindelwald's search for Credence, and tells him the boy is in Paris.

work begins with Stuart Craig's freehand pencil drawings. From there, Foley says, they move to "a white card model so then Stuart [Craig] can play with it a bit." For the more complicated or technical builds, like the steel and glass structure of the Ministère des Affaires Magiques de la France, for example, the model may be digitally rendered or mocked up as a 3-D design. Foley says, "The concept artists work in 3-D and VR so you can virtually stand inside a set piece to get an idea of it . . . It used to be that we would produce the drawings, give them to visual effects, and they would produce the 3-D model and the extensions. Now, we work with them much more closely." Today, the concept artists can start with a 3-D model, refine it, and then give it to visual effects. Once the meat of the design is figured out, the senior art directors break down every detail. Foley says, "That work is then given

A view of one of the cemetery's winding paths.

to our incredibly talented construction team—three hundred plasterers, carpenters, painters, riggers, sculptors, scenic artists —who take the drawings and create the real pieces."

One scene was, in fact, filmed on location: Paris's Père Lachaise Cemetery in the film is actually London's Highgate Cemetery. Foley says, "We went to Highgate and shot there successfully for a few nights. It was great to be on location, and the crew really enjoyed it." Due to rain and general poor weather conditions, however, the location shoot had to be moved indoors. No small feat, the crew re-created the cemetery and the exterior of the mausoleum on Leavesden's largest studio stage, close to where they built its accompanying intricately designed amphitheater. While the Père Lachaise Cemetery

was shot on location in London's Highgate Cemetery, and then at Leavesden, much of the set design for New York City was re-purposed from the first Fantastic Beasts film to become the streets of Paris, and London's most popular landmark attractions were either built on set or created with digital manipulation and special effects.

Eddie Redmayne discusses the scene with director David Yates.

PROP-MAKING DEPARTMENT

French wand boxes.

Dumbledore's Admonitors.

"On a film like this, if there's a material that can't be found or can't be bought, it has to be made. And that's where the prop-making department comes in."
— PROP MAKER PIERRE BOHANNA

The prop-making department works closely with the set-decorating department and the art department to envision and design in-world props, from cauldron handles to stunt suitcases. Unusual for big-budget blockbuster films, the Harry Potter series and now the Fantastic Beasts franchise largely rely on tactile props. The more grounded the set looks, where the actors can interact with the props and their surroundings, the more realistic everything reads on-screen. Magical elements, like flying broomsticks and mythological-looking beasts, are then afforded a sense of realism, too. When audiences first visit the Circus Arcanus in Paris, there's a plethora of magical creatures and fantastical happenings, such as magical penny whistles in a variety of animal shapes.

This sense of realism translates into the smallest of details. In creating some of the props featured in 1927 Paris, the team aimed to make everything look and feel of the period, even down to the screws. Prop modeler Emily Bick explains, "We had to think a bit more about what was invented then." In the 1920s, screws were flat only, and the team consciously designed around that fact. Or, take another common object: suitcases. Bick says, "Back then, suitcases were made with pressed cardboard or with leather. So we created molds and cast them out and tried to imitate those materials . . . I ended up using sheet wax and texturing the wax to make it look like leather or pressed cardboard." Bick made suitcases for Queenie and several different scene-dependent versions of Newt's case. (Newt's hard-edged case, for example, was replaced with a softer, lightweight version for chase sequences.) For Queenie's suitcases, she made two sets of interiors—one with several cosmetic pockets inside and another even fancier version, all the better to convey Queenie's sense of style and femininity. By comparison, Newt's case is bruised and battered, worn in. Keen viewers may note that Newt's case is different from that of the first film. Besides looking more weathered, the case now has a secret pocket on its side. "I think that's top secret," Bick says. The prop-making department has made countless other cases, too, many of which are used in stunt scenes. Beck says, "Some stunt cases are made out of foam, so very soft, so someone can be hit over the head with one. They can also be quite hard, and that's so someone can stand on them. It depends on the stunt. Sometimes, a suitcase will be quite lightweight and won't open—that way the case won't fling open if the stunt calls for someone to throw it. Or they can be animatronic." The department made several animatronic cases—ones that open automatically—for the last film.

Within the prop-making department, there are several teams. From the modelers to the molders to the painters and all the trainees in between, every single prop in the film works its way down an assembly line of trained and talented artists. By the time a prop is in its finished form, virtually everyone—or at least every subsection of the prop-making department—has handled and helped to create it. The design process for propmaking is varied. Concept artist Molly Sole explains, saying, "Sometimes we'll come up with ideas and do a few mock-up designs to show to [production designer] Stuart [Craig] and we'll discuss which direction we should take the design. And then sometimes Stuart's got a completely different approach, and we'll go away and work up something along the lines he suggested. And sometimes, it's just a found prop." Grindelwald's skull pipe, for example, was a prop Craig had discovered but repurposed, cracking its jaw and adding various effects to make it look darker, off-kilter, and more sinister. To create the massive moon in Dumbledore's Defense Against the Dark Arts classroom, however, the team first did a metal etching, adding all sorts of fine detailing to it, like craters and lines. Then, they hand-painted the metal with a paint base to which they added acid. The acid ate through everything but the

Concept art rendering of the circus big top.

The interior of Newt's case.

paint, leaving behind a craggy pattern on the face of the moon. Actor Jude Law, who plays Dumbledore, says, "I've never been on anything quite as big as this. The sets are magnificent, and they, along with the creatures—and everything else—helped me do my job. When you're in a classroom that is for all intents and purposes a real classroom, with the details and the props, it makes that little leap of imagination very easy." By virtue of painted backdrops, Law says he could even see the view when he looked out the classroom windows, a detail that certainly helped the actor visualize where he was in the scene.

Handiwork from the prop-making department shows up in virtually every scene and on every set. Bick says, "The thing with this job is that you don't necessarily do one thing. You work on a project with several parts that a lot of people had their input on . . . It's a team effort. Not one person ends up making one thing." From creating the massive telescope in Dumbledore's Defense Against the Dark Arts classroom to making sure the paint on the Parisian newspaper stands looks authentic and of the period, the prop-making department is a world of wonder unto itself.

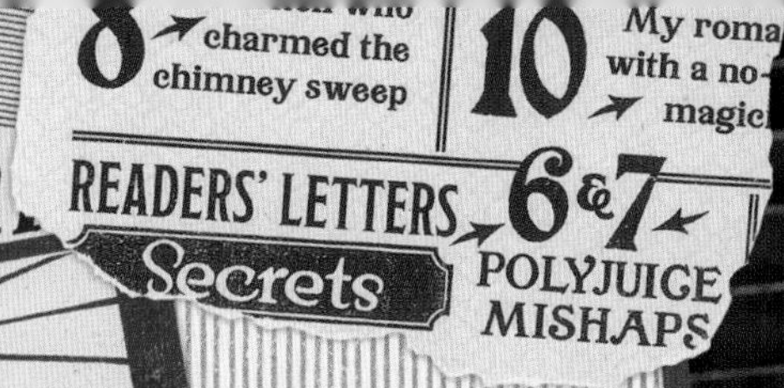

ROYAL S.

NEW YOR

ROYAL STAR STEAM C.

8 → charmed the
chimney sweep

10 My roma
with a no-
magic

READERS' LETTERS
Secrets

6 & 7 →
POLYJUICE
MISHAPS

Eye drops for
Mooncalf.
3 drops/Nightly.

Don't forget to feed
the Niffler!!

"Newt is so full-hearted and passionate and brilliant." —ACTOR EDDIE REDMAYNE

Newt Scamander's life revolves around fantastic beasts. Newt's mother bred Hippogriffs; the possibility of working with beasts was an all-encompassing idea of Newt's from an early age. Even when he attended school at Hogwarts, he looked after an injured raven chick. As an adult, Newt maintains a menagerie of rescued beasts in the basement of his South London home. Actor Eddie Redmayne says, "I think it was something in his blood."

Newt believes that nothing that happens in nature is unnatural. Nature itself, as it truly is, is essential. Redmayne says, "He believes that these creatures are just misunderstood. If you really get under the skin of how they exist and what their habitats are and how they behave, we can learn a great deal from them." This message of conservation—and of caring for, protecting, and observing other species—speaks to Newt's core sense of compassion and empathy. But, as producer David Heyman observes, "I don't think the beasts in the title are just the beasts themselves. I actually think the film is also about the beasts within."

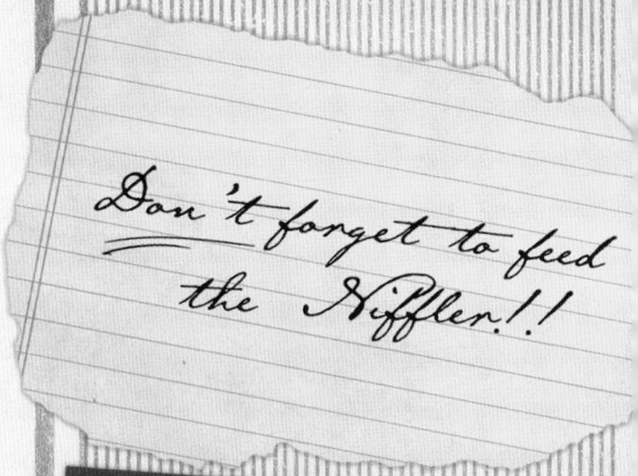

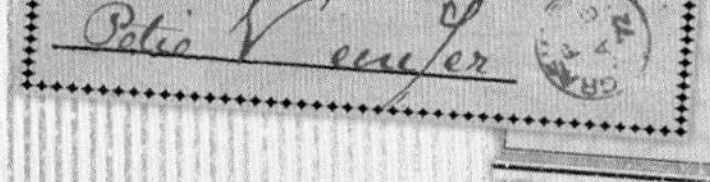

N°29
Petie Vendor

NEWT SCAMANDER

"Newt's in a very different situation, and he's being challenged in other ways
than he was in the first film." —DIRECTOR DAVID YATES

Newt Scamander is an atypical hero. He's socially uncomfortable and isn't particularly good with people. "But," says Eddie Redmayne, "that doesn't make him easy, and that's what I love about Newt: he's not easy." Despite the uneasiness and discomfort Newt may wreak upon himself or cause in the lives of the people around him, he remains true to himself. "He's not trying to please anybody," Redmayne says. He continues, saying, "In this film, audiences see him with Dumbledore . . . They have a great master-apprentice relationship, but even then, I think the qualities that Dumbledore always saw in Newt that were unique were his complete authenticity and his refusal to bark to other people's notions of what 'normal' should be." In the first film, Newt nonetheless successfully befriended Tina Goldstein, her sister, Queenie, and Jacob Kowalski—each outsiders, too, in their own way, and fighting their own personal demons. "It's through their relationships with one another," Redmayne says, "that they further themselves and find the beginning of the path toward happiness, love, and contentment." In *The Crimes of Grindelwald*, audiences witness the evolution of these characters' relationships with one another.

For Redmayne, it wasn't difficult getting back into character despite a year's hiatus from filming. He says, "There's something interesting about working on J.K. Rowling films—their reach is so far it's like we never leave. The character sort of burns inside you a bit. So an ember of Newt is sitting there, and I get to return to playing a character I've played before, but also with

the same band." While the film revolves around the looming threat of Grindelwald's beliefs in the triumph of pure blood and his desire to bring wizards and witches out of hiding to rule over the non-wizarding community, Newt's journey is just as important. Both men are on the search for Credence, and Newt's (mis)adventures eventually lead him straight to the belly of the beast as he—and his friends—confront Grindelwald. Redmayne says, "Jo [J.K. Rowling] creates these wonderful characters and then puts them in incredibly complicated situations and demands that they fend for themselves: they fight for their morals, they fight for what they believe in, and they make choices. And, for me, this film is about Newt going from being an individual to realizing that he actually has to make a choice and join a team." Newt, being a natural-born lone wolf, learns how to join the pack.

Newt's wildly successful book *Fantastic Beasts and Where to Find Them.*

NEWT'S STYLE

"When you read J.K. Rowling's script, there's so much color and vibrancy in it—so many tones." — ACTOR EDDIE REDMAYNE

While Newt still favors the same silhouette, his manner of dress is more urban and polished than it was in the first film. As he is a newly successful author, his clothes look a tad more grown-up. Costume designer Colleen Atwood says, "His shell is a little slicker." Atwood designed the costumes themselves to be flexible and loose: Redmayne's physicality is key to his portrayal of Newt Scamander, so much so, in fact, that his costumes have stretch fabric incorporated into certain areas of the seams that aren't visible to the eye. Atwood says, "If he wants to bend over strangely or pick up a creature, he isn't all of a sudden frozen in space because his costume's too tight."

Newt's sense of physicality was present on the page: in the first film, J.K. Rowling wrote Newt as having a unique walk and, as Redmayne says, "something Buster Keaton–esque to him." This bit of direction was particularly helpful to Redmayne; as an actor, Keaton has a specific physical presence. In the scene where Newt drinks Polyjuice Potion and "becomes" his brother, Redmayne made the physical transition appear effortless by adopting the way fellow actor Callum Turner walks and moves as Theseus. Redmayne also adopted a certain physicality when he had scenes with any one of the beasts: Newt constantly interacts with strange creatures, some of whom also move strangely, and Redmayne played off their movements to showcase the different sides of Newt's personality.

Newt cuts a dashing figure on the streets of Paris.

NEWT AND TINA

"What I love about Tina and Newt is that they're both outsiders, and they're people who don't instantly mesh." —ACTOR EDDIE REDMAYNE

Dear Newt

Sorry it has taken me a while to write. I hope you and all your travelling companions had a safe journey back to England, and that there were no accidental case switches along the way. Work at Macusa is hectic, clean up from the subway incident is more widespread than imagined. We are working around the clock to make sure all memory of the event is erased. I have been reinstated as an auror. So how have you been? How are you keeping after recent events?

I can't help but think of the loss of Credence from time to time, but at least for now we have Grindelwald safely in our custody where he can do no more harm.

Hope to hear from you soon.

Take care of yourself

Tina

> Above: Newt and Tina (Katherine Waterston) at Le Ministère des Affaires Magiques de la France.

Newt and Tina's relationship is . . . complicated. "It's not an easy relationship," Redmayne admits. "They're kind of outsiders who, at the end of the last film, began to find each other and galvanize each other through working together." At the start of the second film, however, their relationship is severely strained, partly because Newt's traveling documents are being withheld by the Ministry of Magic. Redmayne says, "All Newt wants to do is go back to New York, find Tina to give her a copy of his book, and to see her again." And while Newt's absence isn't ideal, it's the least of their problems.

Newt and Tina had been corresponding by mail, sharing their thoughts on the nature of bureaucracy and the Ministry, when Tina's letters stop. Newt believes she's stopped writing because of his harsh opinion on Aurors, of which Tina is one. The more painful truth is that Tina spied a wizarding tabloid magazine that declared Newt had become engaged to Leta Lestrange. Jilted and heartbroken, Tina ceased all correspondence and, worse, began dating Achilles Tolliver, a fellow Auror.

The tabloid article was sensational. Leta was really due to marry Newt's brother, Theseus. Redmayne says, "A large portion of the film is simply about two people who keep missing each other, and who eventually find one another. And, what's interesting is that even though they start the film at loggerheads, subconsciously they're brilliant at working together . . . Their relationship is drawn not through words but by an almost sixth sense to look out for each other." The characters, both seemingly socially uncomfortable and inhibited, nonetheless have a keen sense of intuition and work best when they're in a crisis together. Katherine Waterston, who plays Tina, says, "They're both a little awkward and shy in some ways but really thrive in high-stakes, dangerous situations. Some people go kind of foggy in a crisis, and these two people, they get clearer." If only they could apply that same kind of clear-headedness to their own relationship.

SPELLBOUND

No.0224
1927

Celebrity Secrets & Spell Tips of the Stars!

Prestigious NO-MAJ SOPRANO IS VEELA IN DISGUISE!

FLEAMONT POTTER'S POTIONS *enchant* THE SALONS!

Shameless GINGER WITCH TRUE IDENTITY REVEALED!

a Shooting Star: CHILD PRODIGY CELESTINA

BEAST TAMER NEWT TO WED

Bachelor magizoologist Newton Scamander to marry childhood sweetheart! *sensational story* ☞ PAGES 4 and 5

The BRILLIANT QUILL PRIZE

POLYJUICE *Mishaps* → **Secrets**

Stars ← PISCES & LEO *what a pair!*

nominees revealed!

WEEKLY EDITION 22125A 1927

The wizarding world isn't without its splashy tabloids: *Spellbound* erroneously reported Leta Lestrange's impending marriage to Newt Scamander. The mix-up left Tina Goldstein feeling jilted and proves there's no substitute for good journalism.

NEWT'S HOUSE

Concept art for Newt's neighborhood in London.

Actor Eddie Redmayne says, "One of the things David [Heyman], Jo [J.K. Rowling], Stuart [Craig], and I discussed was: does Newt sleep in his apartment? That didn't make sense to me. He's a man much more at home traveling through the jungle or out in the field. It made much more sense that he would have lived out of his case for the year he spent collating information for his book *Fantastic Beasts*." As a result, Newt's South London flat is intentionally stark. It's only when audiences witness the beast hospital downstairs that they get the full breadth of Newt's personality.

INTRODUCING
BUNTY, NEWT'S ASSISTANT

"One of my favorite new characters in this film is Bunty." —ACTOR EDDIE REDMAYNE

BUNTY'S WAND

Bunty's wand isn't as extravagantly designed as some of the others, but it still captures the essence of her personality. Dedicated, earnest, and diligent in her job as Newt's assistant, Bunty is a woman of simplicity and integrity. Sole says, "I wanted to do something organic for her." Though it may be difficult for the casual moviegoer to see, Bunty's wand is covered in hand-carved leaves; they wind around the handle. It's a small detail, but one that emphasizes Bunty's authenticity and grounded personality.

Played by British actress Victoria Yeates, Bunty is Newt's assistant who has a soft spot for her boss and helps him care for the magical creatures in his basement. Redmayne says, "When I read about Bunty in the film, I said to David [Yates], 'I wonder what the backstory is with her.'" Within a few days, J.K. Rowling presented the team with a fully fleshed-out short story about Bunty and how she and Newt first met at Newt's book-signing party for *Fantastic Beasts and Where to Find Them*. A longtime fan of J.K. Rowling's writing, Yeates says she's not only honored to be part of the series but considers the films' core messages to be important. She says, "In these films you're really getting to see what we go through, the beasts within us, and what we have to overcome to become the people we want to be."

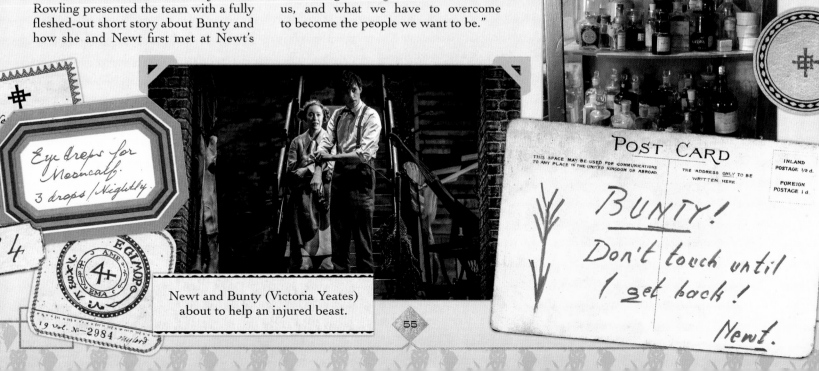

Eye drops for Mooncalf. 3 drops/Nightly.

Newt and Bunty (Victoria Yeates) about to help an injured beast.

POST CARD

BUNTY! Don't touch until I get back! Newt.

THE BEASTS AND THE MENAGERIE

"The Niffler is back. Pickett is back."
—VISUAL EFFECTS SUPERVISOR CHRISTIAN MANZ

Beneath Newt's home, at the base of an Escher-like staircase, is a mind-boggling menagerie: a hospital for damaged creatures. Redmayne says that "walking on that set is pretty breathtaking." To give the menagerie a feeling of magic, production designer Stuart Craig set the basics—the room's flooring and bricked archways—and then exaggerated the scale of the space. The staircase itself is cantilevered out of the wall. In a real building, such a staircase would collapse but, as supervising art director Martin Foley says, "the magic is there, so you believe it." A nod to the Potter series, the stairs are reminiscent of Hogwarts' magical moving staircases. Smack-dab in the middle of the menagerie is Newt's shed, which in the first film, was inside his case.

To outfit Newt's menagerie, set decorator Anna Pinnock visited ZSL London Zoo and had a look around its veterinary department. The decorating team then transposed much of the zoo's supplies—old and modern—and cast them into Newt's world. "A lot of it was very much as they would do in the zoo today," Pinnock says. "Bits of string and pipe and cardboard, things they use to improvise medical equipment for animals . . . we tried to incorporate much of the same." The majority of the furnishings and equipment in Newt's menagerie, however, are of a more wizarding nature, and had to either be created by the art department or revamped. Keen viewers will note, for example, that Newt's operating light resembles a 1960s-style light fixture and that's because it is, in fact, just that. Pinnock explains, saying, "We just added things to it, and that's what's so much fun . . . to add earlier period detail to something that's from a different era." A mash-up of 1960s-style design and early 1900s décor, the operating light looks wholly original and befitting a veterinary office, albeit a magical one.

Creating the beasts that inhabit the menagerie required hundreds, if not thousands, of designs from both the art department and the visual effects department. Producer David Heyman says, "Gradually we would cull them and bring them down to the ones that we were most excited about. And that was just the beginning. We didn't want the beasts to be designed

Newt's basement—home to his menagerie of beasts—is cozy and welcoming.

Newt's wall of tools, used for tracking and catching beasts.

Newt and Jacob Kowalski
(Dan Fogler).

Newt's eyedropper, from which he administers medicine to a Mooncalf.

in isolation. Movement was essential. So we began doing animation tests." These rudimentary tests let the filmmakers see how each creature's movement or style of movement would best communicate the creature's personality. The visual effects team works closely with the filmmakers on the animation tests to make sure each creature's movements are fluid and realistic-looking. The puppeteering department then matches the work done by the visual effects team.

Supervising creature puppeteer Robin Guiver says, "I guess our work as puppeteers isn't so different from the work as actors in that we're dealing with something that has a personality, emotions, motivations." Guiver and the rest of the puppeteering team spoke with the visual effects team as well as the animators and the concept artists to get a better sense of where the beasts came from and how they might move. They then researched and referenced real animals, drawing inspiration from their similarities as well as their differences. For a creature like the Kelpie, which is described in Newt's book as taking the form of a "horse with bulrushes for a mane," and based on a mythological creature from folklore, the team had to decide how much of the Kelpie's movements would be similar to that of a horse. How does the undulation of being in water dictate the beast's movement? Guiver and his team simultaneously explored the underlying emotionality of the scene as well as Newt's relationship to the beast, asking questions like: Does the beast trust Newt in that moment? Does it not trust him? Is it aggressive? Or is it friendly and affectionate or playful? Making these emotionally based decisions helped the team decide how the Kelpie would move, and how they could best manipulate that physicality, working in tandem with the visual effects and art departments, to bring the creature to life.

A FAMILY OF NIFFLERS

"There's not only one scene stealer; there's now an entire family of scene stealers."
—ACTOR EDDIE REDMAYNE on the baby Nifflers

Baby Nifflers.

While every beast in Newt's menagerie is unique, the Niffler stands out as a fan favorite. Bursting with personality, the Niffler is small and cuddly, intelligent and mischievous. The Niffler may be small, but he makes a big impact. For *The Crimes of Grindelwald*, the filmmakers and the visual effects team were charged with creating a whole family of Nifflers. While the creatures themselves are rendered in CGI, the puppeteering department creates stand-ins so the actors have something to play off. Depending on the scene requirements, the team uses differently constructed puppets. Supervising creature puppeteer Robin Guiver says, "We've got puppets that have little rods in their heads they're really good at looking and interacting and making eye contact. We've got ones that are on the ends of sticks that can run around very fast for the camera to follow and for us to work out exactly what their patterns of movement are. We've got ones that really are just like big, weighted black bean bags" so that if actors need to interact with the creatures, they can pick them up. There's a heft to what they're holding, and this helps the actors envision the creatures as being real. It also helps the animators— they can see how the skin of the creature should react when it's being held or touched.

Don't forget to feed the Niffler!!

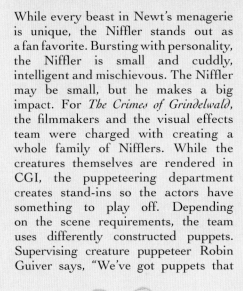

SHEET 1 of 13

Balance Chart

DATE: *April 1927*
CREATURE: *Niffler*
ILLNESS: *Swallowed a galleon*
TREATMENT: *Rest, stomach rubs & revival potion*

DAY / OF ILLNESS	1		2		3		4	
	AM	PM	AM	PM	AM	PM	AM	PM

APOTHECARIO
— London —

ELIXI

Mixed with My...
Do not feed to Ni...

Balance Chart

MOONCALVES

Beloved by cast and crew, the Mooncalves make a reappearance in the second film. Shy and with large eyes, long necks, and four spindly legs, the Mooncalves are nocturnal by nature and emerge from their burrows only to gaze at the full moon. In an especially tender moment, Newt is seen caring for one by administering eyedrops.

AUGUREY

The Augurey—a bird with greenish-black feathers—leads the camera around Newt's menagerie, darting about and following Jacob and, in the process, giving audiences a (literal) bird's-eye view of the space.

A VFX rendering of the Augurey beast.

Eddie Redmayne tending to a Mooncalf stand-in. The visual effects department adds the final computer-generated beast in postproduction.

KELPIE

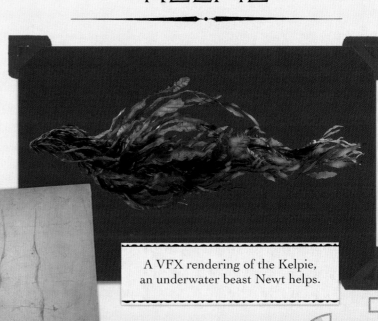

A VFX rendering of the Kelpie, an underwater beast Newt helps.

phoenix comparative
lengths — research
further

PICKETT

In severe cases administer ...
under beasts tongue.

DO NOT FEED TO THE BOWTRUCKLE

"Working with CGI beasts is hilarious. It's totally bizarre. It's as weird and as odd as you'd imagine it to be." —ACTOR EDDIE REDMAYNE

Pickett is a Bowtruckle, a creature that stands at a maximum height of eight inches and is mainly found in England, Southern Germany, and parts of Scandinavia. So miniscule he can fit inside Newt's pocket, and often does, Pickett frequently assists Newt. Adept at picking locks, Pickett has helped Newt get out of more than one dicey situation. Redmayne admits that Pickett is his favorite beast, saying, "Newt has a soft spot for him. I have a soft spot for him. I love the new baby Nifflers, but they cause a bit of havoc for Newt. Pickett's just so small and twiglike and sweet." For being so small, Pickett has an outsized personality that complements Newt's own vulnerabilities. Producer David Heyman says, "For me, the two most successful beasts in the first film were the Niffler and Pickett because they had the most personality. Pickett's reticence and awkwardness were reflected in both the design and the animation."

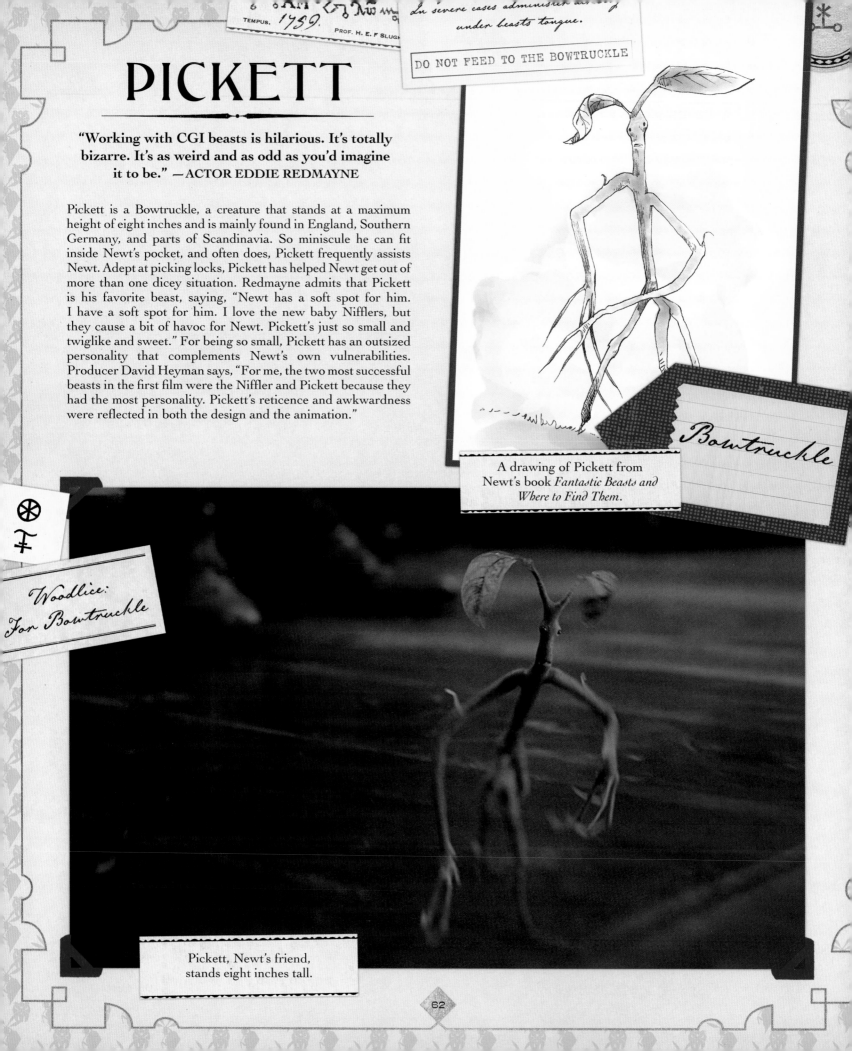

A drawing of Pickett from Newt's book *Fantastic Beasts and Where to Find Them.*

Bowtruckle

Woodlice: For Bowtruckle

Pickett, Newt's friend, stands eight inches tall.

JACOB KOWALSKI

"He's fun to dress . . . His costume becomes clothing very easily." — COSTUME DESIGNER COLLEEN ATWOOD on dressing Jacob Kowalski

Sherlock and Watson. Laurel and Hardy. Newt and Jacob.

In *The Crimes of Grindelwald*, fan favorite Jacob Kowalski resumes his role as Newt's dear friend. Jacob and Newt play opposite sides of the spectrum — physically as well as personality-wise — from each other. Dan Fogler, the actor who portrays Jacob, says of their relationship: "Newt is book-smart . . . and Jacob's street-smart and more of a people person . . . and so the two of us get together and it's like right side/left side of the brain, and we just work together." In many respects, Fogler's character is the comedic relief, and he and Redmayne share a throwback sense of humor. This is intentional. Fogler explains its origin: "Eddie and I love doing the physical comedy stuff . . . I know that he [Redmayne] incorporated the Chaplin duck walk into his gait. I did the same thing. We're both fans of that era." While Charlie Chaplin and Buster Keaton inspired the actors' humor and physicality, a lot was improvised on the spot. Redmayne says, "I love working with him [Fogler] because he comes with a force of imagination, a force of ideas. He plays stuff. He tries stuff. If it doesn't work, he tries something new, and he always pushes you to a really brilliant and different place."

Fogler says Jacob has "evolved" since the first film. At the end of the first film, Jacob's memory was seemingly

An Augurey joins Jacob as he wanders around Newt's menagerie.

Jacob Kowalski

wiped clean—Obliviated—as required by wizarding law. Despite his memory loss, Jacob creates pastries and baked goods in shapes reminiscent of the very fantastic beasts he was supposed to forget, and he seems to recognize Queenie when she walks into his shop—evidence, perhaps, of his subconscious love for all things magical. Now a successful baker, Jacob's grown up a bit, and his relationships, especially with Queenie, have become more layered and complex. However, when Newt first sees Jacob, he knows something is a bit off. Jacob is over-the-top jolly and high on life—a little too high, even for Jacob Kowalski, a man who doesn't say no to life's adventures. Queenie's put him under a spell. When Newt counters the spell and frees him of her magic, Queenie reads Jacob's mind and, upset, runs off. Though the core of their argument is rooted in Queenie's magical manipulation, their emotional confusion is tangible. "Their relationship dynamics are real," Fogler says, and this is one of the reasons he can readily identify with Jacob.

"The beautiful thing about Jacob," Fogler says, "is that he goes along . . . . He finds himself in the middle of chaos and he's such a good person that he's, like, 'Oh, my God, how did I find myself here? This is insane but, yes, I'll help you until the end of your journey.'" Fogler notes that he, himself, wouldn't be up for the challenges Queenie and Newt offer him, and can't help but feel inspired by Jacob.

With such a big heart, who needs a wand? As the only lead who doesn't have one, Fogler admits, "Yeah, I don't get a wand . . . which is sad since I'm magic on the inside and I've got a soul of gold."

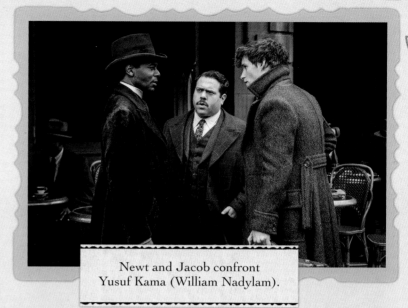

Newt and Jacob confront Yusuf Kama (William Nadylam).

Jacob and Newt at a Paris café.

QUEENIE GOLDSTEIN

"This film tugs at your heart. David [Yates] always talks about keeping our human element at the forefront, and in this film, audiences get to watch these characters as they grow." —ACTRESS ALISON SUDOL

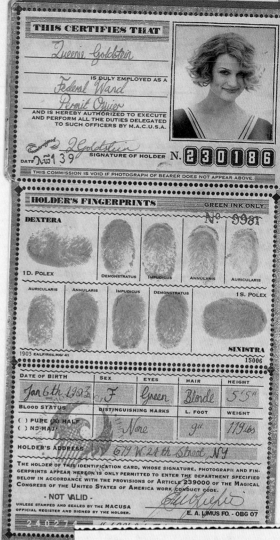

Personal ID card belonging to Queenie Goldstein (Alison Sudol).

Alison Sudol plays Queenie, an American witch and natural Legilimens, and the younger sister of Tina Goldstein. (A Legilimens is someone with the ability to extract thoughts, memories, and emotions from another's mind.) In the first film, Sudol says there was a "real innocence and vulnerability and joy and excitement" to Queenie. She met and fell in love with Jacob and embarked on an adventure of a lifetime. For a character like Queenie—open and free-spirited, compassionate and kind—new love and the raucous promise of an adventure were delightful. By the second film, however, her love for Jacob is under siege. Stringent laws, which have been in place in the wizarding world for hundreds of years, prohibit relationships between wizards and non-wizards, of which Jacob is one. Producer David Heyman says, "Queenie wants to marry Jacob. Jacob is reluctant to do so because of the illegality and the potential consequences within the magical world

and the potential consequences for Queenie." However, Queenie brings Jacob to London under false pretenses. As Sudol says, "Queenie's going to have Jacob whether Jacob likes it or not." Her idea, however, doesn't go according to plan, and Queenie's forced to embark on her journey alone.

On a quest to find her sister in Paris, she's taken by Grindelwald's acolyte, Rosier. Sudol says, "She's scooped up by Grindelwald in what's easily the most vulnerable moment she's had in her adult life . . . The thing about Grindelwald is that he's a master manipulator," which means Grindelwald knows exactly which heartstrings of hers to tug in order to woo her into his dark campaign. "With Queenie," Sudol says, "he [Grindelwald] very quickly understands that the way to get to her is through her giant heart . . . He also reacts to her gift [of reading people's minds]. Queenie's never been told that [her power] is a gift. She's always been shushed and . . . it's been a

frustration, an annoyance, to the people around her, and here you have this intriguing, mysterious man, who sees her as this powerful woman. She's been rejected by Jacob; it's no wonder she gets swayed by Grindelwald."

Sudol admits that she was initially surprised that J.K. Rowling committed her character to a dark storyline. Sudol says, "I think it's an amazing thing that Jo [J.K. Rowling] is taking her down this path where she's going to have to get strong in order to find her way . . . It's a really beautiful exploration of the descent. In ancient mythology, women voluntarily and intuitively know to go to the underworld in order to choose with wisdom how to come back and integrate themselves back into the world."

In the wizarding world, Queenie's power is rare and special, and is but one of the reasons Grindelwald is interested in her. For Sudol, it was difficult playing a normally sunny character who's suddenly not so sunny. Early on in filming, J.K. Rowling gave her a bit of advice, telling the actress to "trust your instincts." From that moment forward, Sudol says, she felt she'd been given permission to explore Queenie's character. "That's a real gift for an actor," Sudol says. The challenge was finding the connective tissue between the first and second films. She says, "I wanted to make you believe that Queenie, at her core, was still the same girl we met in the first film, and that you understand every step she takes in this film, and stay with her. I wanted that most of all—for audiences to stay with her even if it hurts."

QUEENIE'S COSTUME

"The minute I put on this dress it makes me feel good . . . like Queenie!" —ACTRESS ALISON SUDOL

Costume designer Colleen Atwood says, "Queenie has some great looks in this film." As with every character's costume in the film, the attention is in the details. Sudol says, "Colleen is an incredibly detailed and skillful craftsperson as well as an amazing visionary. Her clothing has this extraordinary precision." For this film, Atwood and Sudol both felt that Queenie should present a more sophisticated version of herself. Her elegance is expressed from the smallest details of her brooch to the tip of her wand. "What I love about Queenie's wand," Sudol says, "is something I love about her costumes and her character, which is that there is a great deal of beauty to it but it's simple as well . . . It just feels good. It's got a lovely weight at the end but it's very delicate at the tip."

Sudol specifically requested plaid for Queenie's costuming. She says, "I just felt like Queenie would come to London and go, 'Well, what do they wear in England? Hmm . . . I think they wear tartan so I'd like to have an outfit in tartan.'" Atwood sourced tartan-inspired fabric from Berlin, which she had redesigned in colors better suited to Queenie's personality and the film's overall palette. Together, Atwood and Sudol settled on a beautiful, one-of-a-kind brooch—in the shape of a moth or butterfly—as the accessory de rigueur. The piece of jewelry speaks to Queenie's character transformation, and is intentionally ambiguous. Is it a butterfly or is it a moth? Sudol may describe Queenie best, calling her a "butterfly of the night."

Queenie at Le Ministère des Affaires Magiques de la France.

Queenie Goldstein

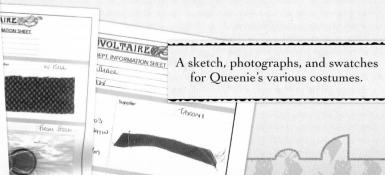

A sketch, photographs, and swatches for Queenie's various costumes.

The visual effects team creates atmosphere for Newt and Dumbledore's London walk.

Composition for which elements of the Paris streets will be digitally created.

> "Stuart [Craig] designs the world, and we then bring his world to life."
> —VISUAL EFFECTS SUPERVISOR CHRISTIAN MANZ

Visual effects supervisors Tim Burke and Christian Manz work closely with David Yates, along with a crew of concept artists and animators, to design the progression of certain action sequences and to help develop certain characters—like Pickett—who depend on digital effects for their cinematic livelihood. The visual effects team uses J.K. Rowling's script as their springboard and begins collaborating immediately upon reading, sharing ideas with the filmmakers and producers, who provide feedback. This back-and-forth process goes on for months prior to Yates shooting even one frame of the film, and it continues well into postproduction. In this sense, says Manz, "visual effects is in a fairly unique position of following the story from the very, very beginning all the way through the

end . . . only the director and producers come on that same full-length journey." Because the visual effects department is present throughout every stage of the filming process, the team gets to collaborate with virtually everyone—from stuntmen to every level of the shoot crew to the postproduction houses.

"For this film," says Burke, "we're trying to bring in a bit more magic . . . So, you'll see sequences where we're establishing that this wizard world is actually living in parallel and you can walk through spaces in Paris where you think you're in a normal environment, and then you pass into a wizarding world, and you realize, a little bit like platform nine and three-quarters, that these two things exist in parallel." To create this parallel world, the visual effects department would usually depend on the green screen. However, much of the set work on *The Crimes of Grindelwald* is beautifully rendered and physical; many of the backdrops are hand-painted and the sets themselves are fully constructed buildings. This, says Manz, makes the design work for visual effects much more tangible. "What makes these films work," he says, "is that we're not in the green room. We've got something physically there that we then build on. For the scenes in Paris, we're actually able to grab buildings from there and build digital versions of them." To do this, a crew films streetscapes, and other real backgrounds, that the visual effects department then renders in CGI. "We use a system called Ncam," Manz explains, "which enables you to look through the viewfinder and see all the stuff that isn't there." This is incredibly useful for Yates and director of photography Philippe Rousselot, who use the CGI renderings and the Ncam to have a better idea of what the city actually looks like when filming certain sequences on set. (The set, for example, may only have a streetscape; the CGI rendering "fills in" the Eiffel Tower so Rousselot understands how the camera needs to pan off the sky and onto the Tower before honing in on the streets below.) Yates can then line up natural-looking shots that won't have to be reframed later.

The visual effects team also works in pre-vis, that is, low-stock animation, to block out certain scenes, especially those in which beasts may be featured. Animator Blair McNaughton says, "We use it [pre-vis] to figure out how we want to shoot the scenes, figure out any interaction that might need to happen between the creatures and the actors . . . In post-vis, we put a bit more refined animation on top of the plates . . . and once everything's approved, it'll go into final animation, where we can polish the creature work." Pre- and post-vis are also used for working out key sequencing moments—the high-velocity chase, for example, at the start of the film—that might be carried out in CGI. Manz says, "We put cameras in, actors in, and work out how an action scene might play out," which helps free up David Yates and J.K. Rowling to concentrate on other aspects of the filmmaking process, like the dialogue or the narrative of the story itself. By the time the director and the film crew are ready to shoot a scene, the visual effects department already has a thorough, working knowledge of how it will be laid out, including what works and what doesn't. The team can also apply rough visual effects to the pre-vis so the editor can work with rough versions of action sequences, the creatures and their environments in plates, or anything else that may be layered with CGI.

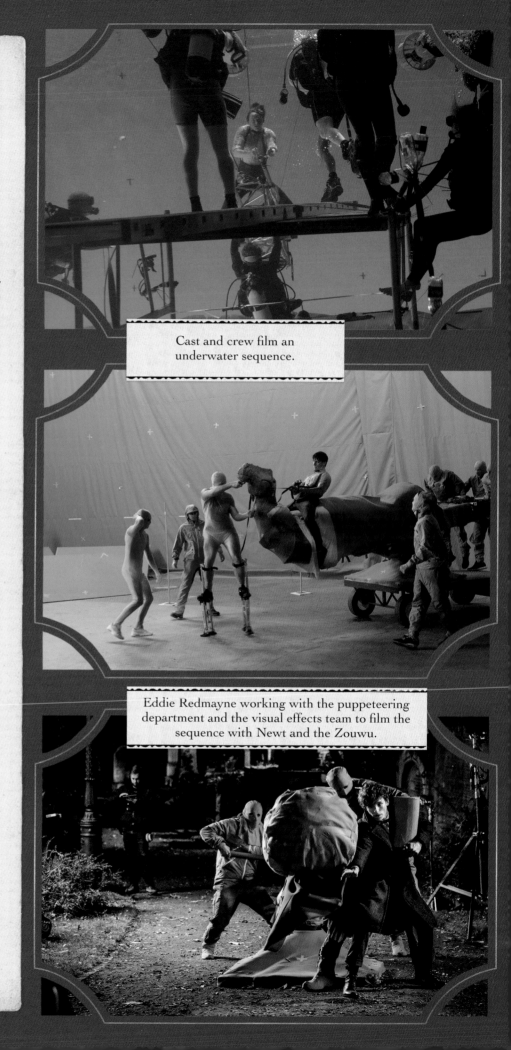

Cast and crew film an underwater sequence.

Eddie Redmayne working with the puppeteering department and the visual effects team to film the sequence with Newt and the Zouwu.

PORTKEY TO PARIS

"This film is a different beast. Literally. The last one felt like an adventure. This is a thriller." —ACTOR EDDIE REDMAYNE

The Portkey was first introduced in the Harry Potter series. An enchanted object, a Portkey instantly transports anyone who touches it to a specific location. So as not to draw the attention of non-wizards, a Portkey is usually a common, everyday object, like an old boot (used to transport groups of wizards and witches to the 1994 Quidditch World Cup) or a statue (used to transport Harry Potter from the Ministry of Magic to the headmaster's office in Hogwarts). In *The Crimes of Grindelwald*, Newt pays the fare of fifty Galleons to use an illegal, rusty bucket Portkey to transport himself and Jacob from the White Cliffs of Dover to Paris — a handy yet risky way of getting around his travel ban.

Newt and Jacob prepare to travel by Portkey.

The Portkey: a rusty bucket.

"One of the biggest beasts is probably Paris."
—VISUAL EFFECTS SUPERVISOR CHRISTIAN MANZ

Credence comes to Paris, France, on a mission to discover the truth about his personal identity. Queenie's in search of her sister; Newt's in search of Tina; the British Ministry of Magic is looking for Newt; Jacob's looking for Queenie; and Leta, preferring to keep the truth about her family under lock and key, wants to prevent people from digging too deep into the Lestrange history. For the cast and crew, having the storyline set in Paris, 1927, afforded a unique creative opportunity to materialize sets, costumes, props, and visual effects that were a magical interpretation of the period. Everything looks like Paris in the 1920s and, then again, it doesn't.

To truly understand the city—its architecture and buildings' interior design; its signage; even the quality of its light—the crew visited the French capital, walked its neighborhoods, and studied its history, and then returned to Warner Bros. Studios Leavesden in the UK and re-created what they saw. Like most industrial cities in the 1920s, Paris was grimier and grittier than the polished streets and gleaming architecture that exist today, and the production departments could exercise a fair amount of control by building the city themselves. They could also repurpose some of the sets of New York City, which had already been built for the first film, as well as build according to specs that would allow the most room for the cameras—and their attending rigs, etcetera—to move about freely. Producer David Heyman says, "Paris: it's a beautiful, extraordinary place. But one thing that David [Yates] does, I think so brilliantly, is that the magical world does not feel separate or apart—it feels organic to the real world."

NEW YORK CITY TO PARIS

"They're not just beautiful sets. They're more than that. They're intelligent sets."
— DIRECTOR OF PHOTOGRAPHY PHILIPPE ROUSSELOT

Much of the set for New York City—its streets and building facades—had already been constructed at Leavesden for *Fantastic Beasts and Where to Find Them* and, so, for its sequel, the art department didn't have to reinvent the wheel. In fact, the team used some of the same sets from the first film, transforming the gridded streets of New York City into the quaint, winding cobblestone sidewalks and roads of late 1920s Paris, France.

Supervising art director Martin Foley says, "Manhattan is famously a grid [of streets]. Paris isn't a grid. It has all kinds of lovely intersections with five routes combining into one. Streets crisscross one another . . . So Stuart [Craig] took the grid and added a couple of really distinct slices, and we added elevation, and steps, and slopes." By any measure, the set for the main streets of Paris is large—over eight hundred feet. The team also repurposed some of the facades from the New York City set.

Behind the scenes, the streets of
New York City.

Each storefront, brownstone, and New York City sky-scraper is reclad and converted into Parisian architecture. "By the fifth film," Foley jokes, "there will be five sets of facades, one in front of the other." While some of the changes are wholesale, others require more specificity. Because Parisian windows are much more detailed and smaller than those used in American architecture, every single window was resized and set. This sense of detail also comes into play with the graphic elements of the signage that fronts store windows.

"The difference between going from New York to Paris," says décor and lettering artist Julian Walker, "is that the Parisian streets are much narrower, much smaller. There's a lot more going on in the turns. In the first film, when we were in New York, we had a bunch of hanging signs. That was where all the lettering came from—it was designed to sell product." And, ideally, to do so in as little amount of space possible. Being much older than New York City, however, Paris is a bit more refined, and the signage of the shops reflects this wizened flair. In the film, the wizarding world is alive and well in Place Cachée, a shopping district that is a shift away from the non-wizard world, where everything—from the storefronts and their window displays to their wondrous products and customers—conveys a sense of the magical. There, Walker says, "all the elements people already know of the wizarding world come into play."

New York City's facades and streets got a
makeover to become the streets of Paris.

PLACE CACHÉE

"It was so very exciting to see Paris come to life on our back lots." —EXECUTIVE PRODUCER TIM LEWIS

The cinematic version of Paris in *The Crimes of Grindelwald* is a composite of real world and make-believe. From the non-wizarding community's viewpoint, there's nothing more to Paris than what meets the eye: the city's wide, gorgeous boulevards are sprinkled with secret alleyways that lead to pint-size patisseries and romantically nostalgic *boulangeries*, the on-set versions of which were filled with actual loaves of bread, croissants, and buttery desserts. Another Paris exists, however: a world that can only be seen and experienced by witches and wizards. To gain entry into this magical world and all its beguiling shops and stores, witches and wizards pass beneath a tall statue, and the non-wizarding shops transform into wizarding ones. This shopping district is called Place Cachée. Actor Eddie Redmayne says, "One of the things that always intoxicated me about J.K.

Eddie Redmayne surveys Place Cachée.

Rowling's world was this idea that you can peel something back and discover a more vibrant, magical, brilliant world beneath it all . . . It's an exciting escapist idea." The shops that line the wizarding streets are meant to pay homage to Harry Potter's Diagon Alley but are also unique to the French cityscape. If everything—from the sweets store and the apothecary to the clothing boutiques and the Quidditch supply shop—looks real it's because, for the most part, it is. From the hand-molded sweets to the specially created volumes that line the shelves of the wizarding bookshop, the set is incredibly detailed and more magical than Paris is itself.

M. Sanfin
PRIX 72 ß

K. Rammelle

K. Rammelle

CONFISERIE K. Rammelle ENCHANTÉE

K

SUBLIMES
BONBONS
DÉLICATS

An up-close look at the French sweets and treats handmade by the prop-making department.

A collection of all things Quidditch as sold by one of the French wizarding shops.

ÉQUIPEMENT QUIDDITCH

GASTON

38

McAARON

DEPUIS 1392

38

GASTON McAARON   DEPUIS 1392

38   ÉQUIPEMENT QUIDDITCH   38

ÉQUIPEMENT   QUIDDITCH   BALAIS

McAARON

GASTON McAARON

LE CORBEAU MYSTIQUE   ANIMALERIE   HIBOUX ET OISEAUX

Bz

CM

LE CORBEAU MYSTIQUE   ANIMALERIE   HIBOUX ET OISEAUX

LUNA ☾ AURORE
JUMELLE

5.50 Bz

La
Marque
Préférée
des
Sorcières
Élégantes

Dr. AZIZ
BRANCHIFLORE
De l'apothicairerie du Dr. Aziz

Dr. AZIZ BRANCHIFLORE

· SORCIER ·

SUPERBEMENT QUALIFIÉ

· INSECTOLOGIE ·

· TRAITEMENTS par les FEUILLES VÉGÉTALES ·

· BAUMES de REPTILES ·

35

P
Petites Potions
Fabricants d'elixirs de qualité
Essence de Folle
MANIPULER AVEC SOIN
221

P
Petites Potions
Fabricants d'elixirs de qualité
Eau de Miel
MANIPULER AVEC SOIN
121

This shop specializes in only the
highest-quality ingredients for potions.

36 BAGUETTES MAGIQUES 36

PARIS COSME ACAJOR 1614

A sketch of a window dressing for
the local wand shop.

ORME 3558
PARIS
COSME ACAJOR

COSME ACAJOR
VIGNE

PARIS COSME ACAJOR

LA LICORNE
PARISIENNE

LA LICORNE
PARISIENNE
BLEU DE CORBEAU
FABRIQUÉ EN FRANCE

NOIR

31
ACAJOR
PARIS

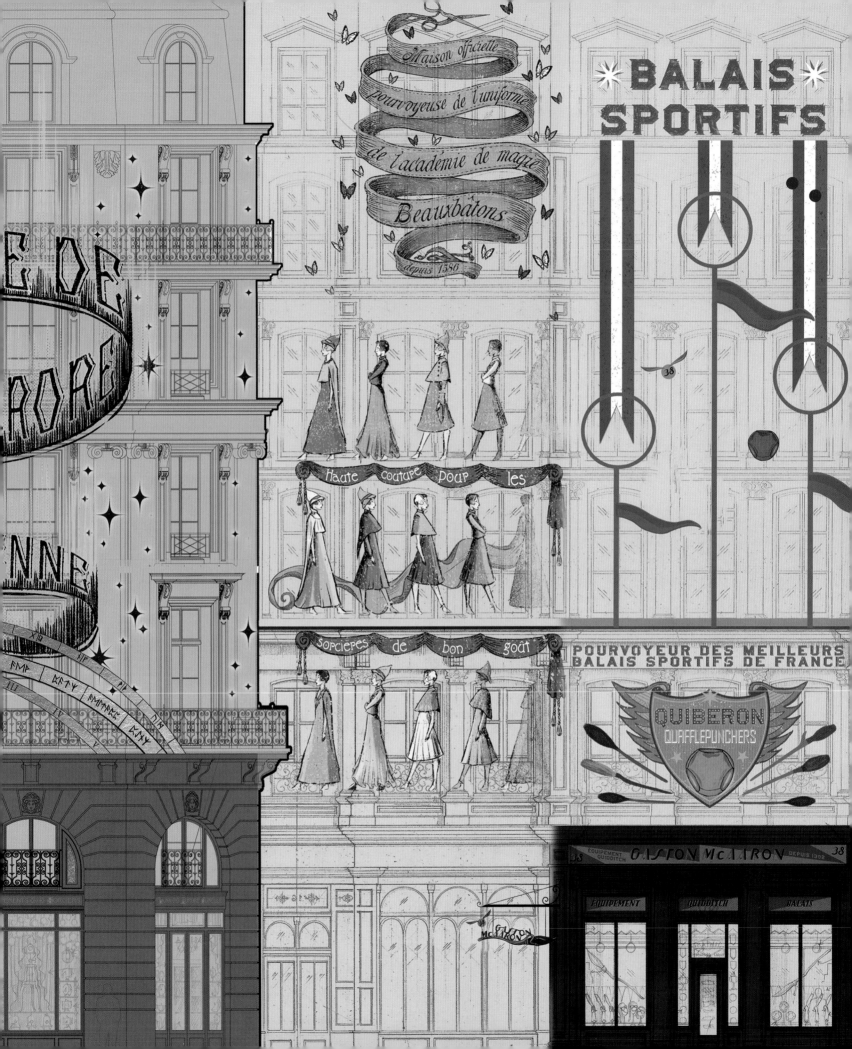

CIRCUS ARCANUS

*"I don't think anyone is jaded about these extraordinary sets. Every single time
we see a new one, our jaws are on the floor."* —ACTRESS KATHERINE WATERSTON

Circus Arcanus is one of the film's darkest places. Full of Underbeings and caged creatures alike—the Zouwu and the Oni, included—the circus speaks to the horrors of entertainment as spectacle. While there are moments of genuine magic that inspire childlike amazement—for example, life-size bubbles that children can float around in—Skender, the ringmaster, can be cruel, and Credence knows it's not the best place for him nor for the Maledictus. Supervising art director Martin Foley says, "It's quite mean-spirited. Outside it's all joyous and everyone's having fun, but these Underbeings, these creatures that find themselves as the center of attention there, are actually quite sad. It's a moving part of the film." This sense of darkness is reflected in the costumes as well. "I consider the Circus Arcanus less of a circus and more of a rough kind of freak show," says costume designer Colleen Atwood. She says, "Everyone's costumes were poorly designed; they were shredded and falling apart. They had a little bit of cheap sparkle to them, but it was a kind of low-rent circus, and the characters wearing them all had a sadness to them. Instead of being a happy circus, it's much more blue and noir."

Circus-goers congregate
outside the big top.

The scenes that unravel in the circus involve a huge amount of visual effects. So much of the set design, as set decorator Anna Pinnock says, "has been led by David [Yates] and the visual effects department, coming up with ideas that they feel like are valuable in terms of all the acts." The spectacular fire that engulfs the circus—just as Tina and Kama get close to Credence—was created by the visual effects team, and is an apt visual metaphor for the underlying currents of the film itself.

CIRCUS TREATS

Circus programs, ticket stubs, and labels for a variety of potable concoctions.

The set for the entrance to the big top circus tent.

INTRODUCING SKENDER

"Skender's a kind of people trafficker, and he's quite entertaining and scary."
— DIRECTOR DAVID YATES

Skender, played by American-born Icelandic actor Ólafur Darri Ólafsson, wears several hats: beast trainer, showman, ringmaster, and owner of Circus Arcanus. Despite these job titles, costume designer Colleen Atwood says, "He's more complex than what a normal ringmaster is, who's typically a gigantic announcer and a man usually from theater opera. Skender's not from that world. He's from a darker place."

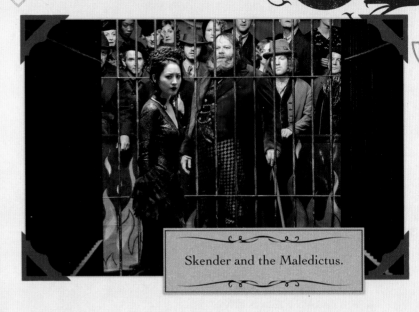

Skender and the Maledictus.

SKENDER'S COSTUME

"Skender is his own ringmaster. He's a combination between an animal trainer and a ringmaster, so he's got a dark edge to him."
— COSTUME DESIGNER COLLEEN ATWOOD

Skender looks every bit the showman dressed in his costume. A classic ringmaster's coat is red and tailed, and finished with a top hat. For Skender, costume designer Colleen Atwood slightly altered the traditional lines of a ringmaster's coat and soured the color of its fabric. She says, "He was fun to dress because he's just a wonderful personality and he's a big man. Some people can just put on clothes and make them special, and Ólafur is that kind of person. We had a great time collaborating with him; he can sell a costume and really inhabit it."

Skender (Ólafur Darri Ólafsson) looks every bit the circus master.

INTRODUCING
THE MALEDICTUS

"The Maledictus is amazing." — DIRECTOR DAVID YATES

A Maledictus is the carrier of a blood curse that destines an individual to ultimately transform into a beast. A featured act at Circus Arcanus, the Maledictus has a unique storyline, one that's deeply personal to the character's transformation. Director David Yates describes her story as "how she tries to cling to her humanity in the brief time that she has" before her transformation into a snake is complete.

The Maledictus and Credence meet at Circus Arcanus, a place of sadness and abuse. Claudia Kim, the actress who plays the Maledictus, says, "The Maledictus is a prisoner in this place and there's another layer to it, too, because she's also bound to be a prisoner in her own body. So [the circus] is this place of great hopelessness . . . and I think Credence's desire to find out who he is—that drive, the determination—gives her hope, and so the circus is really the beginning of their journey." Speaking about their relationship, actor Ezra Miller says, "There's real love between them. They're both struggling in similar ways . . . and they're thrust into a situation wherein they're codependent and within that they're trying to figure themselves out." The Maledictus has a soft spot for Credence and advises him that no one, not even Grindelwald, holds the answer to his most burning question. She tells Credence, "He knows that you were born, not who you are." When the Maledictus escapes the circus along with Credence, it's like she's shed her old skin; with the sudden rush of freedom comes a sense of partnership and the possibility of healing. Kim says, "Credence brings out the woman in her. She becomes nurturing and protective."

To bring the Maledictus to life, Kim was keenly aware that her body movement would do a lot of the talking. Kim incorporated the serpentine into her performance, elongating her gestures to suggest a slithery quality. Supervising creature puppeteer Robin Guiver observes, "There's a lot of undulation

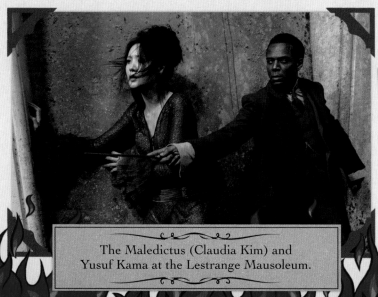

The Maledictus (Claudia Kim) and
Yusuf Kama at the Lestrange Mausoleum.

in even just how she walks around and moves, generally, and that movement of the spine translates beautifully into the serpentine role." Her manner of dress was important, too: Atwood outfitted Kim in a lace, tango-inspired dress screened over with metallic foil to convey the impression of snakeskin without literally using snakeskin. Atwood says its design was based on research on tango dresses but then "pushed into the fantasy aspect of the character." Ruffles line the bottom edge of the dress and along its sleeves to depict the coils of a snake. For her snake transformation, director David Yates turned

to the talents of his visual effects and puppeteering teams. Guiver says, "We've got a fantastic twenty-foot-long snake." The puppeteering team uses this model as a visual reference for most scenes involving the Maledictus. Actors interact with the model, and the visual effects department layers in CGI later.

The Maledictus straddles two worlds: that of human and that of beast. She's one of the only characters not to have a wand. Kim says, "She possesses a different magic entirely; her instincts are her greatest strength."

THE UNDERBEINGS OF THE CIRCUS

"The circus is the most tragic and dark place where these misfits of magical beings are captured by the horrible and abusive Skender." —ACTRESS CLAUDIA KIM

The Zouwu cage, assembled at Warner Bros. Studios Leavesden, UK.

No big top circus would be complete without its performers and, in the case of Circus Arcanus, the Underbeings who inhabit the circus — half elves, half goblins, half trolls — are without powers but possess magical ancestry. The circus is also populated with other fantastical creatures/performers like Firedrakes, dragons that hiss sparks to combustible effect, and other notables.

ZOUWU

"The Zouwu has had a lot of iterations. It's one of those creatures that takes a while to get right."
—SUPERVISING ART DIRECTOR MARTIN FOLEY

VFX rendering of the fiercely fantastical Zouwu.

The Zouwu is a Chinese beast reminiscent of a cat or a dragon. The size of an elephant, it's also massive, and can run one thousand miles in a day. The beast comes with a backstory: initially part of the Circus Arcanus, the Zouwu suffered years of mistreatment and, as a result, is scared and unsure of its own strength. Supervising creature puppeteer Robin Guiver says, "It's been injured and hurt and treated very badly. Despite the fact that it's a magical beast, there's a reality to that story that we can all relate to . . . Newt recognizes this. So when he meets it, and it's ferocious on the bridge, Newt sees through the Zouwu's ferocity to the fear inside it, and fortunately knows how to get it to a safe place in his case." When audiences next see the Zouwu—as Newt and Tina are escaping from the Records Room in the Ministère des Affaires Magiques—the beast and Newt have bonded.

Depending on the scene, filmmakers relied on different types of puppeteering and technical methods to film Newt with the Zouwu. Sometimes Redmayne would rehearse scenes with a massive puppet mounted on a nine-foot pole that the puppeteers would manipulate. Once Redmayne understood how to interact with the puppet, the scenes would be filmed; the empty space of where the puppet had been would be filled in with CGI. The puppeteering team also made a version of the Zouwu with a very soft foam head that could be touched and pushed. "So," Guiver says, "when Newt gets off the stunt rig he's riding on, he can physically interact with the Zouwu, too." It was important for Newt's scenes with the beasts to look real; while his interactions with humans are sometimes reserved, his personality shines through in his interactions with the beasts.

CIRQUE ARCANUS

KAPPA

The Kappa—a magical water demon—was mainly created using CGI; however, the crew also relied on several low-tech tricks, like using a cardboard cut out as a stand-in for the creature. (The cutout was later digitally layered with CGI.) Sometimes, both methods were used at the same time. Supervising creature puppeteer Robin Guiver says, "When the young circus handler scrubs the Kappa, one of our puppeteers simply held up a big plastic chair so he had something real to scrub against." The special effects team then digitally replaced the plastic chair with a CGI-version of the Kappa.

Concept art for the circus Graphorn.

ATTENTION
CREATURE ONLY TO BE HANDLED BY A QUALIFIED MAGIZOOLOGIST

FIREDRAKE

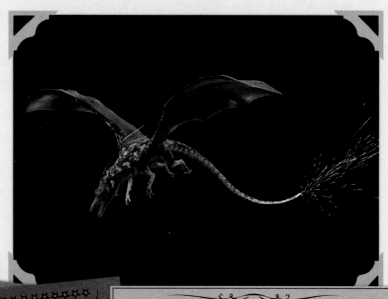

VFX rendering for the Firedrake, a dragon-like creature known for its sparks of flame.

CIRQUE ARCANUS
MUSÉE DES CURIOSITÉS VIVANTES
BIZARRES
SOUS-ÊTRES MAGIQUES
VOYEZ DE VOS PROPRES YEUX LE...
KAPPA

ADMISSION
POUR UNE PERSONNE
TICKET D'ENTRÉE
CIRQUE
N° 1672
POUR UN: ENFANT

ONI

When J.K. Rowling described the Circus Arcanus to actor Ezra Miller, she mentioned that there would be all sorts of creatures assembled there, including a Japanese Oni. A hulking figure with horns growing from its face and mouth, the Oni is also equipped with sharp claws. Rowling says, "The Circus Arcanus is a brutal place. It might seem at first glance to be a place of great wonder and mystery, but in fact, it's a combination of freak show and a form of people-trafficking." If the Oni's appearance telegraphs anything, it's that the circus—at least this one—is the kind of place where sharp claws come in handy.

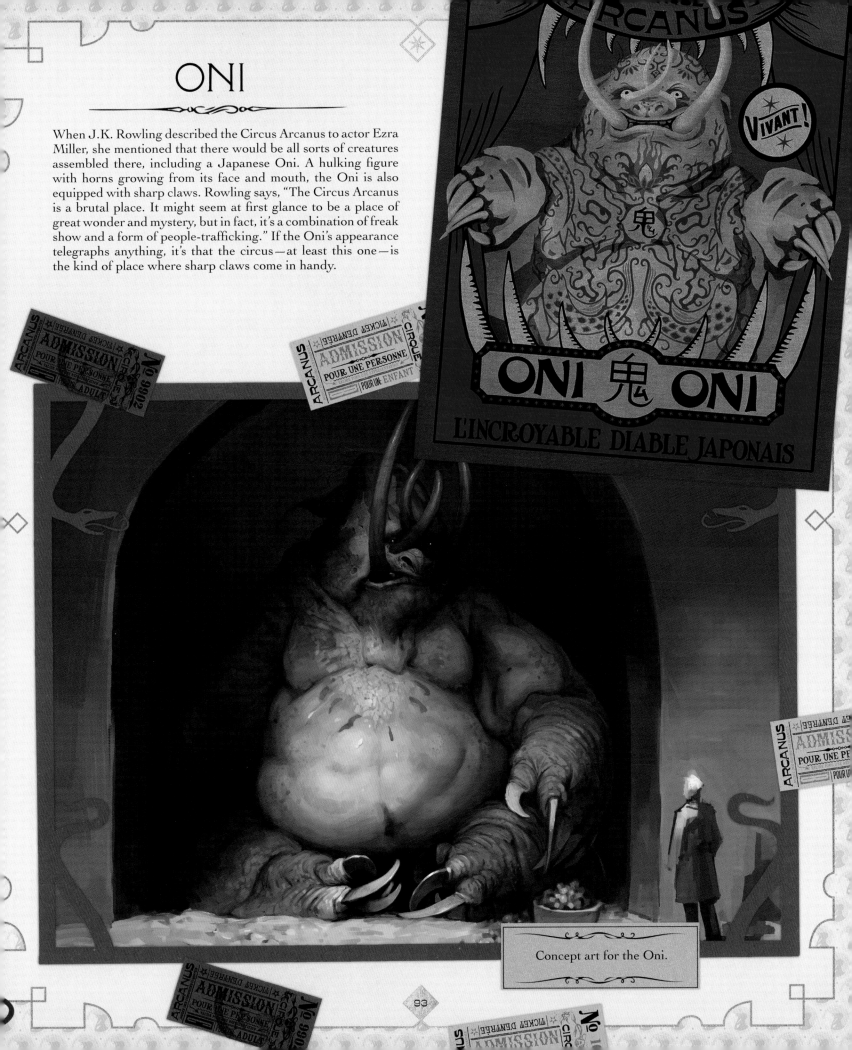

ARCANUS

VIVANT!

ONI 鬼 ONI

L'INCROYABLE DIABLE JAPONAIS

Concept art for the Oni.

TINA GOLDSTEIN

"One of the great joys for me is getting to work with her [Katherine Waterston].
She has such a rigor to the way she works. She challenges." —ACTOR EDDIE REDMAYNE

Tina's Auror agent ID card, front and interior.

M.A.C.U.S.A
★★★
AUROR
AGENT No.240274
Federal Auror Bureau

VALIDATED BY
M.A.C.U.S.A.—REGISTERED

MAGICAL CONGRESS OF THE UNITED STATES OF AMERICA

AUROR I.D. CARD
FEDERAL AUROR BUREAU

Tina Goldstein is a character largely directed by her own instincts, which are time and time again proven to be right. Following her instincts in the first film led to the arrest of Grindelwald and in the second film, she's put to the test once more. While her core sense of self is intact, her confidence is still being restored; a good thing, too, since an Auror needs her confidence as much as her trusty wand. A lot has changed between the first film and the second but Tina's mission remains the same: protect Credence. Katherine Waterston, the actress who portrays Tina, says, "A child in need is her Achilles' heel . . . At the end of the [first] film, she gave him her word that she and Newt would protect him and she's not one to go back on her word."

THIS CERTIFIES THAT

Porpentina Esther Goldstein
IS DULY EMPLOYED AS A
Auror.

AND IS HEREBY AUTHORIZED TO EXECUTE
AND PERFORM ALL THE DUTIES DELEGATED
TO SUCH OFFICERS BY M.A.C.U.S.A.

P. Goldstein
Countersigned   SIGNATURE OF HOLDER   N. 240274
DATE *023S.

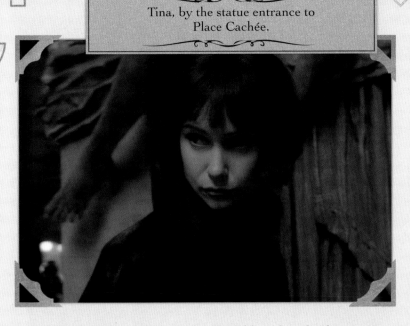

Tina and Queenie, her sister, are at odds with each other over Queenie's relationship with Jacob, a non-wizard. Waterston says, "I felt like I carried the fracturing of their relationship throughout this whole story. It's an extraordinary loss for Tina and I think it explores an important lesson about dealing with and confronting the troubled relationships in your life. If you assume that you can do it later, you may not have the chance." Both women are strong-willed and stubborn, two qualities Waterston says may have contributed to their impasse.

In addition to her strained sibling relationship, Tina's also struggling in her relationship with Newt, mistakenly believing that he is engaged to Leta Lestrange. She's hurt, he's confused, and the combination is a burden on their already awkward relationship. Luckily for them both, there's nothing a good adventure can't solve.

"When we finished the first film," Waterston says, "I thought what a gift that we'll get to return to this world . . . But what surprised me was that . . . it still felt incredibly fresh and, in many ways, like a whole new experience because they've brought in these new, wonderful actors that really take the story in a different direction." New actors also meant new collaborations and the possibility of further character development; Tina, while always grounded, certainly seems to have settled further into herself. Having been reinstated as an Auror, she's more stable in her profession, though she's still unafraid to work around the system whenever necessary to crack a case.

Costume designer Colleen Atwood picked up on Tina's hard-boiled noir-ish sensibility and matched her wardrobe with her evolving personality, trading up the tan trench coat from the first film to a sweeping blue leather coat with a cinched waist. Always ready to be on the move, Tina still favors slacks over dresses and skirts. Atwood says, "Tina stays in that coat [the whole film], but it's the best coat you've ever seen. It's beautiful blue leather and we're all quite fond of everything about it, except how much it weighs. It's quite heavy, but it has a great silhouette and surface . . . She looks like a real detective."

Credence Barebone

Movements November
1926

Nov. 16th N.S.P.S. church

Exit with younger
?? children (possibly siblings)

Nov. 21st   PIKE STREET ①
↓
CHERRY ST. ②
↓
MONROE ST ③

BARCLAY ←
& PARK PLACE

*
M.A.C.U.S.A
??

Dec. 26th.
Boards cargo
ship
SS. ONDINE   Bound for PARIS, France.
Suspicious CIRCUS ARCANUS activities = connection ?

Chastity DIED

? Modesty
? Adopted also ?

Children of
MARYLOU BARE-
BONE

? { BURBONE
BARBON
BEARBANE } ?

DIED
*

Nov. 30th

Searched records
at. N.P.V.S =
Need to return
Dec. 12.

Search Dept. of Health
Division Vital Statistics
for CERTIFICATES

INTRODUCING
YUSUF KAMA

"I'm completely trapped in this character because he's so close to me." — ACTOR WILLIAM NADYLAM

Like most of the cast, William Nadylam, the actor who portrays Yusuf Kama, didn't know which film or what role he was auditioning for—director David Yates kept the specifics under wraps. When he landed the part, Nadylam says Yates "welcomed me into the [filmmaking] family" with open arms. Nadylam emphasizes this sentiment, saying, "I will not forget that word—family—because that's what it is."

Yusuf Kama, like Nadylam himself, is a character who also dwells on the notion of family. A French African of Senegalese descent and the son of a great wizard, Nadylam says Kama "doesn't exactly know who he is. He's basically on a quest for his identity." Because of an incident from his past, he has lost

Yusuf Kama, standing at the entranceway to the Lestrange family mausoleum.

his entire family, and is forced to seek vengeance on behalf of his father. Nadylam says, "His father's desire becomes his . . . Instead of giving him an inheritance of happiness, he gets this inheritance of vengeance. And his life will be dark from that point on."

Kama is on a quest to answer some of life's most complex and universal questions. Nadylam says, "He's a really fascinating character, complex and sophisticated, with an inner struggle. Nothing is white or black for him. He doesn't exactly know who he is. Who are we? Who do we think we are? Do we belong to the family? Do we belong to our culture?" As it turns out, Kama and Tina are both in search of the same person; Kama's personal adventure dovetails with Newt and Tina's journey and puts him on a new trajectory where, Nadylam says, "he'll find out that things are not exactly what he thinks they are."

KAMA'S COSTUME

"We need some magic."
—ACTOR WILLIAM NADYLAM

For Kama's costume, David Yates briefed Colleen Atwood by saying, "Make him look like he's had the best clothes in the world and he's still wearing them twenty years later." The cut and the quality of the fabric for Kama's suit are superb but it's certainly seen better days. The blues and grays of his clothing blend with the Parisian environment so it looks as if Kama is wearing the city itself on his sleeve.

THE PREDICTIONS OF TYCHO DODONUS

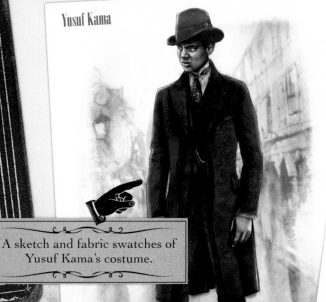

Yusuf Kama

A sketch and fabric swatches of Yusuf Kama's costume.

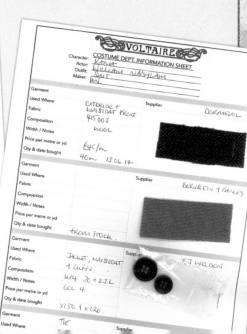

VOLTAIRE
COSTUME DEPT. INFORMATION SHEET
Character: Kama
Actor: WILLIAM NADYLAM
Outfit: SUIT
Maker: hal

Garment		
Used Where	EXTERIOR + WAISTCOAT FRONT	Supplier: DORMEUIL
Fabric	415003	
Composition	WOOL	
Width / Notes		
Price per metre or yd	£45/m	
Qty & date bought	40m 13.06.17	

Garment		
Used Where		Supplier: BERWEEN 9 BANLEY
Fabric		
Composition		
Width / Notes		
Price per metre or yd		
Qty & date bought	FRONT FROCK.	

Garment		
Used Where	JACKET, WAISTCOAT + CUFFS	Supplier: P J WELDON
Fabric		
Composition	WP4 30 + 23 L	
Width / Notes	COL 4	
Price per metre or yd		
Qty & date bought	X150 + x120	

Garment		
Used Where	TIE	Supplier:

KAMA'S HIDEOUT

Located in the Parisian sewer system, Kama's hideout is a dank and secretive place where the mysterious wizard plots revenge for his family's undoing. The film's construction crew built the set in their workshop, closely following the art department's master plans and drawings. They then broke it down, moved it to the studio stages, and quickly re-built it for filming, adjusting elements as needed.

To create the appearance of a sewer, the team tanked water and then built the brick walls surrounding the cavernous water system. The design is in the details: the water is murky, the perfect hiding spot for underwater sewer beasts; the brick is chipped and aged-looking; Kama's personal belongings—documents and notes, his meager collection of books—are nested everywhere. To complete the sense of being underground, the lighting crew and cinematographer illuminated the scene from above, and edged the rest of the set in inky darkness.

Newt gets his bearings inside Kama's hideout.

Kama, overtaken by a seizure, lies immobile on the floor of his hideout.

INTRODUCING
NICOLAS FLAMEL

"An actor's main tool is his imagination. So when you work in this kind of movie, where it's all about imagination, it's absolutely fantastic." —ACTOR BRONTIS JODOROWSKY

The process for actor Brontis Jodorowsky to become Nicolas Flamel is a little alchemistic, which is fitting since the character is based on a real-life alchemist who lived in France during the fourteenth century. Flamel will be familiar to fans of Harry Potter—in J.K. Rowling's world, Flamel was a close friend and partner to Albus Dumbledore in addition to being the maker of the Sorcerer's, or Philosopher's, Stone, a legendary stone that produces an elixir that grants immortality. Not much else is known about Flamel, except that he's lived a very, very long time—six hundred years or so, but who's counting? Jodorowsky says, "I think so many people are excited that Nicolas Flamel is in the second episode of this story. This excitement stems from the mystery of this character. He's the only character who existed in real life."

As a fictional character, Flamel is alive (and mostly well) in *The Crimes of Grindelwald* though Jodorowsky admits it's a genuine challenge to create a character that lives up to fans' expectations. Jodorowsky relied on the script to help maintain his focus on the character J.K. Rowling created. To this end, he used the physical props—and facial prosthetics—to get into character. Makeup took three to four hours daily—a significant

A behind-the-scenes photograph of Nicolas Flamel (Brontis Jodorowsky), the famed alchemist and wizard.

The street sign for Flamel's address.

amount of time for Jodorowsky to contemplate Flamel and settle into his skin, so to speak. "It would be pretentious to say that I arrived knowing the character," Jodorowsky says. "Because you discover the character along with the situations . . . Four hours of prep gives you time to completely get into someone else's mind and this is even stronger, because you really change your face . . . your hair, the wig, everything." Even Jodorowsky's hands are aged. To bring the prosthetics to life and imbue them with a sense of realism, Jodorowsky grounded the character in his body movements. He says, "I'm always trying to find the body of this character and how he would move . . . it's trying to imagine, but it's impossible to know, what it is like to be six hundred years old. What state o

who ha

W immort power he has he mus difficul Wherea he can between types o in seve time co the occa

Flamel, dressed in his centuries-old robe.
The fabric is intentionally distressed
to look ancient.

NICOLAS FLAMEL.
51 Rue de Montmorency
Paris

The Philosopher's Stone,
created by Flamel.

SMELLING
SALTS
COLTON COOPER
PHARMACIES
LONDON
ES29-H98, 1925

NICOLAS FLAMEL'S HOME

To create Flamel's home, the art department took the approach that Paris—and the times—had passed Flamel by. The rest of the city has become more and more developed while Flamel's home has remained a timber-framed, almost Medieval-looking building, outfitted with an old-fashioned studio with stone walls. Supervising art director Martin Foley says, "He's just kind of been left behind." Most of the building's interior walls are warped or bending; the floors have become extremely curved over the years; the stairs are leaning. Foleys says, "Everything has kind of twisted with age."

Flamel's assorted belongings.

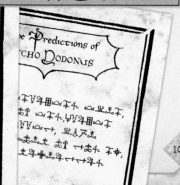

The Predictions of
Tycho Dodonus

102

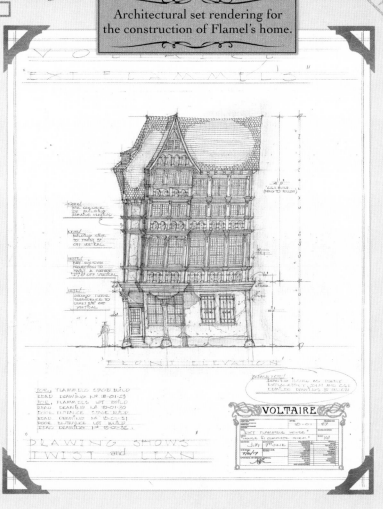

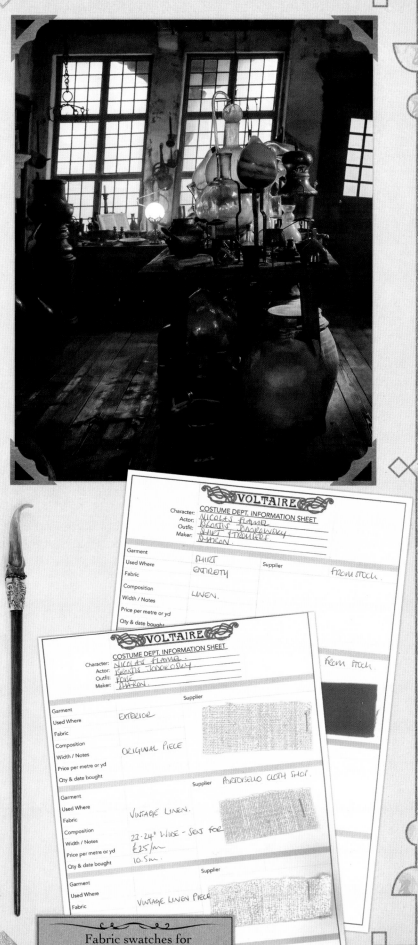

NICOLAS FLAMEL'S WAND AND COSTUME

"For me, as an actor, working on a character is like trying to meet someone. Every day of work, every day of shooting, you know the character a little bit more."
—ACTOR BRONTIS JODOROWSKY

Outfitted with a dragon's claw, Flamel's wand is truly unique-looking. Jodorowsky explains the wand's importance, saying, "Many times in traditional stories, you have a disciple looking for a master when, in fact, it's the master who's looking for the proper disciple. In a way, this [wand] is my master." Where his wand is fairly detailed, his costume is deceptively simple.

In a city where fashion is all the rage, Flamel looks out of step. His sleeves are too long, his shoes are too pointy; his costume isn't tailored to the popular trends of the day. Nonetheless, it seamlessly telegraphs his character. Speaking about the lengthy sleeves, Jodorowsky says, "You immediately get into a physicality because of the length of the sleeves; you need to move with them."

Fabric swatches for Flamel's costume.

A MAGICAL BOOK

"We try to mine as much information from J.K. Rowling as possible." —GRAPHIC DESIGNER MIRAPHORA MINA

Besides his wand and the magic of alchemy, Nicolas Flamel has another tool at his disposal: a magical book, which he uses to connect with his closest confidantes. Graphic designer Miraphora Mina describes the book as a "wizarding utility," comparing it to a wizards' version of WhatsApp, the popular global messaging service. While the conceit of the book is high-tech—and its interior pages are rendered using CGI panels—its exterior is very much of the period. To create it, designers Miraphora Mina and Eduardo Lima referenced Victorian-era photo albums, which were often architectural in form, complete with leather tooling and stamping, debossed effects, hardware (metal clasps or a beautifully decorated security lock), and intricately designed covers. "Because we knew the book was going to be interactive, we thought of it less as a book and more as an object. It's quite structured," says Mina. While she concedes that it could have been made to be much more "magical" in appearance—decorated with crystals and runes or such—that wasn't the point. As a utility, it was essential that the book be both practical and unassuming; a character can simply shelve it in his or her library and no one's the wiser.

The team worked closely with a renowned London-based bookbindery to develop its double-spine design; the book opens down the middle rather than from the side. Each page is hand-stitched and set into the spine so that, when the book is open, the pages lay flat—an essential design component for the CGI panels to function properly. Similar to the hanging portraits in the Harry Potter series, the panels "capture" wizards and witches in situ. (If someone is out, the panel displays their empty room.)

105

PARIS

"Paris of the 1920s was a real melting pot of ideas creatively, artistically, socially. It was a very vibrant time." —DIRECTOR DAVID YATES

Speaking about the set design for Paris, executive producer Tim Lewis says, "It's very grounded . . . We're not designing a fictitious city. We're very much basing the sets on factum, on what existed during the time period." At the same time, he admits, "J.K. Rowling writes about very specific places in her script. It's clear where her research has taken her. We always start off with the script, and make sure that we're sticking to what she's written." Just as Diagon Alley was an important backdrop to the Harry Potter series, so are the rows of patisseries, boucheries, and cafés to this film. The non-magical world of Paris grounds the fantasy world and provides a charming and romantic look at the city during the early 1900s.

Newt and Tina on their way to Le Ministère des Affaires Magiques de la France.

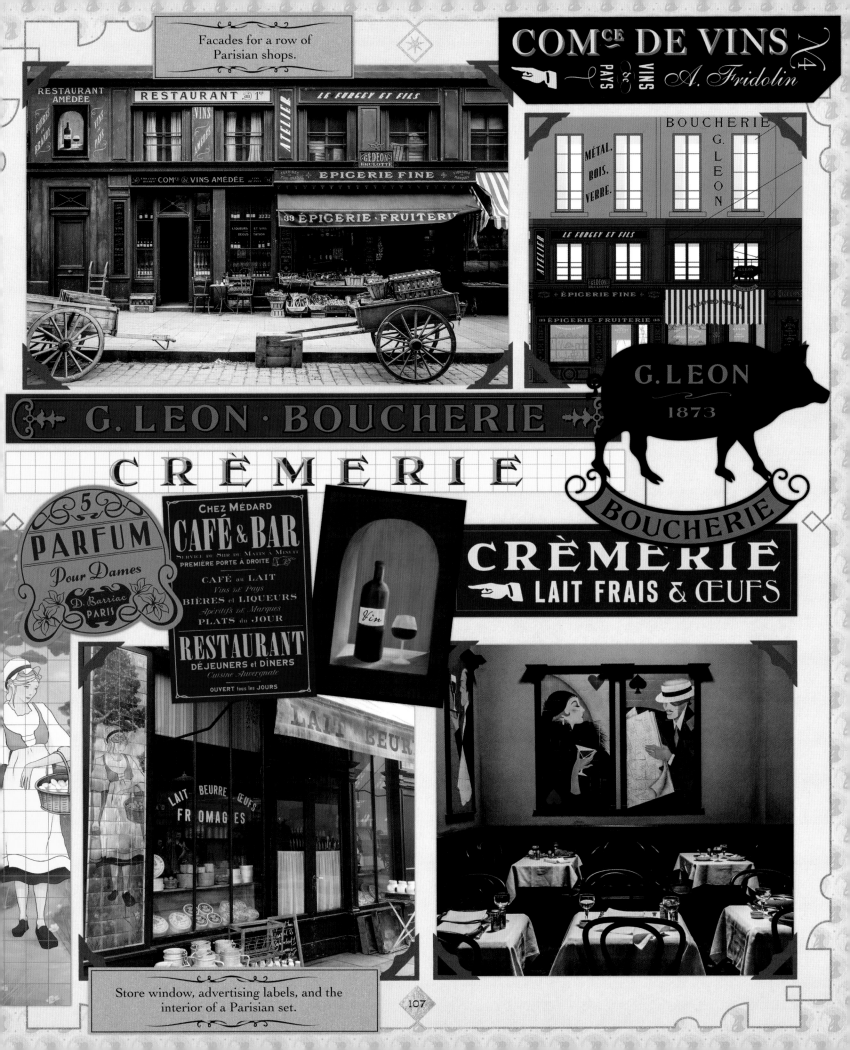

Facades for a row of Parisian shops.

COMᶜᵉ DE VINS №4
PAYS & VINS
A. Fridolin

G. LEON · BOUCHERIE

G. LEON
1873
BOUCHERIE

5
PARFUM
Pour Dames
D. Barriac
PARIS

CRÈMERIE

Chez MÉDARD
CAFÉ & BAR
SERVICE DE SUIR DE MATIN A MINUIT
PREMIÈRE PORTE À DROITE
CAFÉ au LAIT
Vins de Pays
BIÈRES et LIQUEURS
Apéritifs de Marques
PLATS du JOUR
RESTAURANT
DÉJEUNERS et DÎNERS
Cuisine Auvergnate
OUVERT tous les JOURS

CRÈMERIE
LAIT FRAIS & ŒUFS

Store window, advertising labels, and the interior of a Parisian set.

GRAPHIC ART
MIRAPHORA MINA AND EDUARDO LIMA

"As graphic designers, we help tell the story by virtue of any prop." —GRAPHIC DESIGNER MIRAPHORA MINA

Working in conjunction with production designer Stuart Craig, set decorator Anna Pinnock, and the visual effects team, graphic designers Miraphora Mina and Eduardo Lima are an integral part of bringing J.K. Rowling's wizarding world to life. Not only did the duo work on the Harry Potter films, but they've also been on board for both Fantastic Beasts films. From creating Tina's MACUSA ID card and designing the front pages of the wizarding newspapers, to making the wanted posters for both franchises and everything in between, including all the Parisian stores' advertisements and signage (all the way down to the stores' product labels and price tags), Mina and Lima build out anything that has a graphic design element. Their task is vast because the visual world they're working in is far-reaching. The challenge is balancing the graphics of the real world with elements of the magical, and satisfying the cinematic requirements of both.

While working on *The Crimes of Grindelwald*, Mina and Lima often referenced the kind of design systems and language that

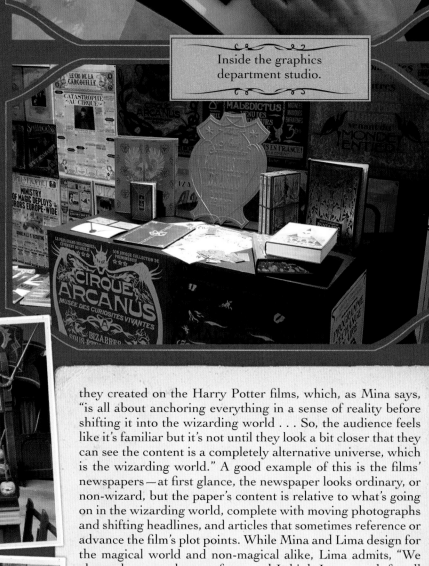

Inside the graphics department studio.

they created on the Harry Potter films, which, as Mina says, "is all about anchoring everything in a sense of reality before shifting it into the wizarding world . . . So, the audience feels like it's familiar but it's not until they look a bit closer that they can see the content is a completely alternative universe, which is the wizarding world." A good example of this is the films' newspapers—at first glance, the newspaper looks ordinary, or non-wizard, but the paper's content is relative to what's going on in the wizarding world, complete with moving photographs and shifting headlines, and articles that sometimes reference or advance the film's plot points. While Mina and Lima design for the magical world and non-magical alike, Lima admits, "We always have much more fun—and I think I can speak for all the departments, even for the actors as well—when you're in the magical world."

To research the look and feel of Paris during the twenties, the team visited the City of Lights and, as Mina says, "tried to immerse ourselves a little bit in the details that no one else is particularly interested in. It's kind of like that's our little indulgence, if you like. So that's anything from typography, advertising, illustrations, printing techniques, and how things would have been manufactured." Those details are then added to the creative palette that the team draws from time and time again to conceptualize their vision. Mina explains,

Graphic designer Miraphora Mina puts the finishing touches on Credence's certificate of adoption.

Graphic designer Miraphora Mina adds aging to *The Predictions of Tycho Dodonus* book.

saying, "We'll try to capture the period by looking at references but obviously we have to create completely new and original material." Much of the typography featured in the film—everything from shop signs to street signs—is actually scanned typefaces from the period; the graphics truly read as being of the time.

The team's strength is in the details. Everything the graphics department undertakes is painstakingly created—right down to the pages of *Le Cri de la Gargouille*, which feature entire horoscopes, obituaries, and humorously titled articles that may or may not make it on camera. No matter—Mina and Lima are nothing but thorough in their design, viewing the graphics as important as any other prop. For this film, the team designed Newt's book *Fantastic Beasts and Where to Find Them*. Made to resemble a book from 1926, the prop is beautifully flamboyant in black and gold—the team imagined how Obscurus Books, his wizarding publishing house, might design it. They also created the wizarding book that Flamel uses: "It looks like a photo album, and when you open it, you can talk to other wizards in your circle," Lima says. And they created the Lestrange family tree. One side of the tree had already been developed by J.K. Rowling, leaving the other half up to Mina and Lima to design. "I've never done that before," Mina admits. "But actually, if you want to make it work, you have to be quite careful." Genealogists. Journalists. Publishers. The graphic design team wears several hats and, luckily for audiences, they do so with aplomb.

DÉCOR AND LETTERING
JULIAN WALKER

Décor and lettering artist Julian Walker takes the work of the graphics team one step further, painting, screen-printing, or stenciling their handiwork onto specific surfaces or props. Walker says, "Obviously, we have a bit of technology where we can generate graphics identically from files. But, ultimately, they [the filmmakers] still want a hand-on-hand feel. We generally use old skills in a modern form." For this film, the team needed to not only create old-world-looking lettering and graphics but also make their handiwork resemble the distinct personality of New York, London, and Paris. In a packed and highly competitive city like New York, "less is more," says Walker. By comparison, the streets of Paris are grander, and the shops' signage can be more refined.

A selection of printed posters for the Paris streets.

WIZARDING NEWSPAPERS

The New York Ghost remains the newspaper of choice for North American witches and wizards. In Paris, however, the most popular is *Le Cri de la Gargouille*, which details all the wizarding news fit to print, with attention-grabbing, front-page headlines like "Catastrophe au Cirque." Designed, once again, by Eduardo Lima, the papers are meant to emulate the look of newspapers from the era and are chock-full of humorous advertisements and serious articles alike.

To create the papers' moving images, the graphics team inserts green screen panels into their design, which the visual effects department then digitally manipulates.

LES GARGOUILLEMENTS FABULEUX DES NOUVELLES FRANÇAISES

LE CRI DE LA GARGOUILLE

Aujourd'hui Plein — Hier Mouillé — Demain Sec — Après-demi Éclipse

2ᵐᵉ ÉDITION DE PARIS · LUNE EN LION · 1927 · Nº 221254 · 25 CENTIMES
Directrice · Danielle Amorinus

Éditorial

LES SORCIERS FRANÇAIS SONT TERRORISÉS

Etupís iò mattis Morbi non sapien nisi sed finibus tempus efficitur a purus sit amet tristique. Mauris tellus arcu, interdum tristique mauris posuerunn, quis et vel quam congue dapibus. Cras risus lorem, fringilla a pharetra at consequat ut nisi. Mauris lacinia sem vitae posue. Cras eu vestibulum libero, a interdum lectus. Donec facilisis porta risus ut lacinia. Suspendisse in nisl sodales, elementum ipsum sit amet, sollicitudin augue. Integer in justo vestibulum ligula porttitor ornare non a orci. Orci natoque penatibus et magnis dis parturient montes, nascetur ridiculus mus. In eu viverra metus. Nulla eget nisi at eros porta lacinia? Vestibulum ante massa, vehicula nec eros ac, luctus elementum odio. Phasellus placerat velit et tristique tempus facilisi. Etiam pretium tempus iaculis. Mauris facilisis dui lorem, iaculis porta nibh congue nec. Maecenas tortor metus, finibus ac feugiat sit amet, auctor eu nibh. Pellentesque placerat urna elit ac egestas massa placerat aliqu.

Éditeur - Maurice Pinho

(Voir la suite 2ᵉ page)

LA SÉCURITÉ FRONTALIÈRE SOUS PRESSION

Dit, et eget sem sagittis, ultrices urna sed aliquam felis. Erat nisl. Phasellus semper, turpis at tincidunt pretium, purus sem, eget venenatis ex sem a dolor. Donec fringilla ligula id mauris ultrices, quis porttitor enim commodo. Nullam ut vestibulum ante. Aliquam cursus mi molestie eros tincidunt blandit. Fusce ut aliquet arcu, iaculis tincidunt eros. Fusce laoreet ipsum. Laoreet bonus, orci eu gravida eleifend arcu erat auctor lectus. Sed vulputate enim nisl et diam. Curabitur gravida tortor et, lectus dignissim facilisis. Sed tincidunt dui in lacinia.

Lmi anus, iaculis a fermentum a, rhoncus vel dui. Aliquam urna nisi, at tincidum purus pulvinar eu scelerisque vel. Donec laoreet a luctus, id blandit mauris imperdiet. Suspendisse id gravida quam, quis efficitur elit turpis a ultricies purus, et turpis. Aliquam at tincidunt dui. Nulla at mauris vel sem iaculis pulvinar. Pellentesque scelerisque nisl ut tristique a bonus, nulla sed dapibus sem scelerisque sem a arcu eget ligula. Vestibulum ante ipsum primis in faucibus orci luctus et ultrices. Cras et fauci ubi ac sed dignissim. Donec at eboni eu dui. Integer molestie dolor a commodo semper. Donec imperdiet urna sed nibh lacinia vitae feugiat dui blandit.

Directrice - Danielle Amorinus

(Voir la suite 2ᵉ page)

Exclusivité

DES SORCIÈRES DE CAXAMBU APPARAISSENT À VERSAILLES

Palais de Versailles

Usperdisse in nisl sodales, elementum ipsum sit amet augue in integer in justo vestibulum ligula porttitor a orci. Orci natoque penatibus et magnis dis parturient montes, nascetur ridiculus mus. In eu viverra metus. Nulla eget nisl at eros porta lacinia? Vestibulum ante massa, vehicula nec eros ac luctus elementum odio.

(Voir la suite 7ᵉ page)

3000 PIÈCES DE MONNAIE TROUVÉES SUR UN NIFFLER À CANNES

il était si lourd qu'il ne pouvait plus marcher!

Ladum convallis, ut ultrices eu iaculis, enim sed gravida, quis elementum dui euismo tellus sed aliquet. In per

(Voir la suite 13ᵉ page)

EN EXCLUSIVITÉ EN EXCLUSIVITÉ EN EXCLUSIVITÉ

CATASTROPHE AU CIRQUE

Département de La Magie - Paris

Abaerba dolor. Maecenas eros ex, suscipit vel lorem in dolor. Ubis mi? Maximus lacus nisl, commodo eget congue sed, eu sapien. Curabitur sed felis a tortor malesuada porttitor ut eu leo. Proin at felis mi. Sed dapibus nibh eget leo interdum, fermentum malesuada nisl efficitur. Proin elementum, amet interdum euismod, turpis quam sollicitudin nisl, ac lacinia neque risus in ipsum. Interdum vel malesuada lacus ac ante ipsum primis in faucibus. Vestibulum rutrum auctor lacus porttitor nisl amet nisi at varius natoque penatibus et magnis dis parturient montes, nascetur ridiculus mus. Nam aerenean leo condimentum rhoncus. Cras at massa ligula. Mauris eu quam erat magna dictum bibendum. Pellentesque vitae odio imperdiet dapibus arcu id, aliquet dui. Maximus id nunc eu turpis efficitur. Vestibulum nec convallis fringilla. Scelerisque pretium tristique risus aliquam fringilla. Pellentesque feugiat sit amet arcu dui aliquet. Phasellus euismod, magna sit amet feugiat luctus orci turpis pretium dui, vitae commodo sem sapien eu sem. Sit urna mattisvel nec fermentum iaculis lacinia gravida venenatis ut risus commodo, tincidunt ipsum in faucibus a est. Vestibulum vel leo ex. Sed sit amet scelerisque felis, ac facilisis nisi. Duis nec risus luctus, mattis eros a nec iaculis est. Duis elementum mi elementum erat amet. Integer quam mi, tincidunt gravida sem in sodales fringilla metus. Donec bibendum scelerisque ipsum non augue a nulla aenean tempus ut sed sapien. Sit amet felis. Integer nibh sem, ultrices at ante sit amet, mollis cursus.

LES CRÉATURES S'ÉCHAPPENT

Phasellus dui cursus neque ut viverra neque et convallis vitae mortis mi, ut ullamcorper justo tristique ac. Quisque rutrum vel enim nec eleifend. Nasce rhoncus mauris et mauris bibendum a, ultricies tortor sagittis. Donec a aenean sed malesuada dapibus. Quisque rutrum vel enim nec eleifend.

H. Lunneaux

(Voir la suite 4ᵉ page)

DES AURORS DE L'ÉTRANGER ARRIVENT EN FRANCE

Département de La Magie - Paris

Lsuscipit. Etiam eu gravida magna. Sed a commodo porta vel fringilla, feugiat vestibulum lectus convallis sed tempor sagittis tristique. Vivamus sem nisl, tempor quis et facilisis venenatis lacus. Phasellus quis urna convallis, ornare eu condimentum quam. Phasellus quis urna convallis. Maecenas nec tortor ac dui tristique sagittis, bibendum nisl necrisus fermentum vitae aenean nisl volutpat. Vivamus at libero ultrices, cursus ipsum non, condimentum massa. Mauris at tortor ipsum. Aliquam vulputate, elit dictum luctus lorem diam massa dui porta sagittis. Cras vel mauris ullamcorper vehicula.

M. Guillory demande aux sorciers de ne pas rejoindre l'armée de GRINDELWALD

Iuisno felis laoreet vitae. Quisque posuere sagittis urna vitae metus sed libero sagittis aliquet. Maecenas at rutrum pharetra ipsum a lacinia sapien. Aenean tincidunt euismod sem et aliquam tellus pretium nec. Cras libero sit amet fringilla suscipit. Duis in venenatis, ligula risus enim vitae eleifend consequat. Duis mattis, lectus ut tincidunt semper, leo est varius leo, vitae auctor enim eu sus vestibulum vestibulum scelerisque. Uti bibendum bibendum facilisis. Morbi ut libero bibendum, eleifend sem tegtbul convallis odio. Mauris rutrum a est et pharetra rutrum. Donec blandit massa porta sagittis. Cras tincidunt sem nec mauris. Quisque bibendum dui id dui bibendum in ultricies magna maximos. Nulla dapibus dol et pharetra rutrum. Donec magna congue erat, et scelerisque eros.

Rosana Hitffelds

(Voir la suite 6ᵉ page)

RECOMPENSE POUR LA CAPTURE

Cirque Arcanus - Paris

Mit purus. Nullam in felis in felis efficitur volutpat. Mortis mi, at ullamcorper justo tristique ac. Cras non massa. Phasellus rutrum vel enim nec eleifend. Quisque lobortis vel metus vitae bibendum. Proin ac sapien vestibulum dictum a rutrum? Vestibulum faucibus cursus odio id pulvinar nibh. Duis et metus eget metus vulputate auctor. Donec augue metus, consequat at condimentum vitae, aliquet odio. Sed vestibulum sem vestibulum lectus vestibulum in ut amet. Integer quam mi, tincidunt gravida sem in sodales fringilla metus. Donec bibendum scelerisque ipsum non augue a nulla aenean tempus ut sed sapien. Sit amet felis. Integer nibh sem, ultrices at ante sit amet, mollis cursus tortor. Donec orci justa, auctor ac faucibus vitae, sodales vitae urna. Donec at interdum augue. Cras luctus feugiat dui, fringilla auctor dolor consectetur eu. In eleifend nunc dolor, eu gravida pellentesque dui. Sed ut blandit felis, a consectetu felis. Pellentesque facilisis, diam vel hendrerit lobortis, risus quam porttitor nulla, consectetur nunc dolor ut velit. Donec sit amet eleifend sem, et tincidunt nulla. Vivamus semper libero et. Maecenas vel ipsum lectus. Pellentesque a scelerisque mi. Maecenas aliquet est blandit massa porta sagittis. Cras imperdiet vitae justo a dignissim erat justo leg.

Luchiane Almeideaux

(Voir la suite 7ᵉ page)

DES MAGES NOIRS SONT PARMI NOUS

Bureau de la Justice Magique - Cannes

Orbieula? Vestibulum a turpis a urna primis in faucibus orci luctus et ultrices posuere cubilia Curae. Aenean ornare ante nec tortor. In eros odio, imperdiet sed interdum finibus, tincidunt vulputate metus? Proin vitae pellentesque lectus. Curabitur et nisl massa. Praesent dapibus consequat. Morbi eu laoreet orci? Vestibulum ac urna ac eros vehicula vestibulum eget at orci. Uti ultricies arcu dolor, eu ullamcorper blum rhoncus eget. Etiam ornare sit amet odio ac sagittis. eget augue pharetra hendrerit in eu, efficitur dui. Suspendisse vel scelerisque nisi, at dapibus quam. Pellentesque sapien leo, scelerisque aliquam et et, malesuada et gravida in imperfect. Vestibulum ante ipsum primis in faucibus orci luctus et ultrices posuere. Donec eunque justo sollicitudin et gravida imperdiet vmo, cumetus suscipit suscipit.

Francesquine Wagnefjeldnee

(Voir la suite 8ᵉ page)

L'Arc de Triomphe n'est pas un portoloin, rappelle le Département de la Magie

gravida ante vel pharetra. Vestibulum luctus velit semper interdum malesuada. Suspendisse metus luctus, ornare dolor nisi.

Martine Machadoux

(Voir la suite 12ᵉ page)

Nouvelles Breves

Un mystérieux serpent géant à deux têtes trouvé dans les grottes de Lascaux

Vestibulum ante ipsum primis in faucibus orci luctus et ultrices posuere cubilia Curae. Pellentesque fermentum aliquam finibus. Nunc dui rutrum eleifend dolor, at imperdiet sapien pharetut. Nulla vitae posuere felis. Integer at ipsum molestie sed feugiat ullamcorper sed dolor. Quisque maximus volutpat tortor ac dapibus ut dapibus a. Aenean malesuada felis odio vitae pharetra eu iaculis ac. Mauris eu malesuada massa. Donec iaculis ornare scelerisque ac velipula. Cras vestibulue tortor facilisis dictum. In tempor laoreet magna. Vestibulum ligula ante cras id gravida in imperdiet leo. Aliquam gravida mi eget mi iaculis.

Cass Nemereux

(Voir la suite 4ᵉ page)

Dernières Nouvelles

Le Bureau de la Justice Magique va publier un pamphlet d'avertissement

Bureau de la Justice Magique - Calais

Elementum volutem turpis quis aliquam a. Erat velit sit bales fringilla et sagittis dui. Pellentesque volutpat nibh posuere felis. Integer at ipsum molestie sed feugiat ullamcorper sed dolor.

MONA LISA OUBLIE DE RETOURNER DANS SON CADRE

J'étais distraite! prétend-elle

Raliquam. Nullam ut eget volutpat, Vestibulum pellentesque nunc elit ante facilisis sit amet varius eget ullamcorper leo. Pellentesque viverra mattis ultricies. Curabitur vestibulum aliquet augue ac urna aliquam.

Alice Tolipanneer

(Voir la suite 4ᵉ page)

SCANDALE DE POTION MAGIQUE CHEZ LES ÉTUDIANTS DE BEAUXBÂTON!

Les œuvres inédites de MALECRIT trouvées dans la grotte des Dragons!

La Grotte - Avignon

Dia ut feugiat metus enim vehicula odio. Maecenas eros cursus felis tempus, bibendum dignissim sapien suspendisse tincidunt rabli at lobortis pellentesque, rably augue cursus elit, pulvinar lobortis leo nisl eget diam. Ullamcorper tempus ultrices. Elit elementum luctus dolor quis iaculis. Vestibulum tempor lacus eget risus euismod nis. Aenean invent ultries, blandit nisl vel lacinia lorem.

Pedro Figueiredos

(Voir la suite 15ᵉ page)

UN CAMEMBERT EMPOISONNÉ TUE UN LAPIN GÉANT

Amollis justo quis elementum dicm. In ac diam dictum, tali a fringitec. Donec eleifend nibh justo. Quisque a umel Diam in sodales erat. Vestibulum nec diam volutpat odio ac lobortis condimentum nisi. Nam

Anne Limonne

(Voir la suite 19ᵉ page)

Faits Divers

LA SORCIÈRE ROUSSE APERÇUE À LYON

(Voir la suite 22ᵉ page)

Un magicien Animagus dans l'affaire du canard

(Voir la suite 17ᵉ page)

Comment contrôler votre grenouille

(Voir la suite 15ᵉ page)

Bref

Mr. Sanfin a importé des chaudrons avec des fonds

lolutpat nunc vel volutpat interdum, nisi ipsum fringilla lorem, eu euismod massa, ord tincidunt metus dolor ut nunc.

Les chapeaux volants s'échappent du magasin Bonnetvolant

aret pretium. Cras eu mattis sed varius et tur ante. Nulla facilisi. Nullam convallis, sapien sit amet porttitor tempus, neque velit euismod massa, ord tincidunt metus dolor ut nunc.

Note Du Jour

Révélation de M.K. RAMMELLE - l'ingrédient secret de mes caramels

Merised. Vestibulum maximd finibus eros mattis aliquet facis. Cras convallis, dignissim ord vitae euismod dius. In sanaugue ac quam euismod a vehicula mattis. Ut leolectus et leo volutpat viverra. Sed mattis quis Mauris a arcu nisl. Curabitur odio nisi, a dictum in. Duis vitae nibh leo, t vel tortor sed risus sagittis, eu, id nunc sodongu ad libero.

M.K. Rammelle

(Voir la suite 7ᵉ page)

«NAPOLÉON ÉTAIT UN MAGICIEN» RÉVÈLE MAGILLARD DANS UN NOUVEAU LIVRE

rutrum in aliquet augue bibendum. Etiam purus purus aliquet at imperdiet a facilisis eget neque. Curabitur molestie nisl et interdum gravida. Aenean non enim at mauris tempus tempus. 7ᵉ page

La Vie Sportive p.12 p.12

Gaston McAaron fait un don d'uniformes de quidditch à de jeunes magiciens

Bulletin Commercial

5 Façons d'économiser vos BEZANTS!

(Voir la suite 14ᵉ page)

Spectacles: Au Théâtres

'JEANNE D'ARC MAGIQUE' p.18 la comédie musicale fascinante commence bientôt

Le Coin de Nicolas Flamel

Les énigmes de l'Alchimie résolues

(Voir la suite 11ᵉ page)

NOTIFICATION DU MINISTÈRE DES AFFAIRES MAGIQUES

AVIS

LA TOUR EIFFEL N'EST PAS UN PORTOLOIN!

ATTENTION!
TOUTES PERSONNES ESSAYANT D'UTILISER LA TOUR EIFFEL À CET USAGE SERA INTERPELLÉ!

AVIS
No. 221254 ELM
MINISTÈRE DES AFFAIRES MAGIQUE DE LA FRANCE

LE COIN DE Tatan Paulette

elit. Class aptent taciti sociosqu ad litora a per inceptos himenaeos. Nunc tincidunt vestibulum vehicula pulvinar nisi nec mattis sed risus sit amet bibendum quis euismod leo. Proin ornare. Aenean porttitor nulla id urna eget consequat vitae, bibendum ex condimentis. Etiam condimentum urna magna ut lorem risus interdum magna, urna ★

docipsum elit faucibus augue, non ornare velit nisl urna non commotis ac sollicitudin velum. Donec vestibulum brevestibulum convallis, id ultrices nibhysat tristique nec faucibus nisl condimentum. Phasellus ac id mauris auctor posuere. Aenean sed gravida lorem. Donec eleifend leo ★

◆ Exclusivité ◆
TOUS LES BILLETS ONT ÉTÉ VENDUS! La pièce 'TO BRIE OR NOT TO BRIE' s'est jouée à guichets fermés

Paris

tincduntelit,eftringillamaurisvellustutorn? Vestibulum sollicitudin eget mi ut, consectetur pulvinar dolor. Morbi viverra tortor in interdum. Duis sed metus ut ante scelerisque euismod in vel neque. Nam eu tempor sapien. Nulla pulvinar id turpis id mattis. Morbi non sagittis nisi sed tibus massa. Vivamus efficitur a purus sit amet tristique. tincidunt metus arcu interdum tristique mauris posuere non. Nulla quis ex vel quam congue dapibus. Donec ut aliquet lorem, rhoncus congue lectus. Cras risus lorem, fringilla a pharetra at, consequat ut nisi. Mauris lacinia servitatae posue. Cras eu vestibulum in rhoncus lectus. Donec facilisis portavitus id ultricen. Suspendisse in nisl sodales, elementum ipsum sit amet, sollicitudin augue. Integer in justo vestibulum ligula porttitor ornare non a orci. Orci varius natoque penatibus et magnis dis parturient montes, nascetur ridiculus mus. In eu viverra metus. Nulla eget nisl at eros ★

UN CHAPEAU RARE DE BONHABILL RETROUVÉ À MONTMATRE

interdum dolibla. Donec recin interdum dui. Nam ed cum erat imperdiet sed iaculis vel ligula. Pellentesque a tellus in erat id luctus neque lacinia vitae. Etiam et tellus acum leo porta gravida dui. Aenean vel pulvinar lacus. Duis dignissim mi tristibus ac. Nunc commotis massa. Aenean ut nulla. Duis bibendum viverra. Vivamus hendrerit dolor vitae villamporper posuere. Sed a elementum nibh. Maecenas congue sapie varius sollicitudin. Phasellus cursus erat condimentum, sodales nunc at sollicitudin ipsum. Lorem ipsum dolor sit amet, consectetur adipiscing elit. Sed ipsum neque gravida a ullamcorper vestibulum. Donec nec erat nisl. Phasellus semper, turpis at tincidunt erat odio dapibus sem, eget venenatis ex sem dolor. Donec fringilla ligula id mauris ultrices quis porttitor enim scelerisque. Phasellum vestibulum ante. Aliquam cursus mi molestie eros ★

10 Bézants de Réduction
pour l'achat de votre nouvel astrolabe en présentant ce coupon chez
LUNA ET AURORE JUMELLE

Donec nec erat nisi erat odio dapibus a ligula id mauris u vestibulum

LES CRÉATURES DES PYRENEES SONT-ELLES REELLES?

Morbi augue. Integer enim justo vestibulum ligula porttitor a orci. Orci varius natoque penatibus et magnis dis montes, nascetur ridiculus mus. In eu viverra metus. Nulla eget nisl at eros porta lacinia? Vestibulum ante massa, vehicula nec eros, ac interdum nibh. Phasellus placerat velit et tristique tempus. Nulla facilisi. Etiam pretium tempus Mauris faucibus lorem, iaculis portasnibh gone porta. Maecenas tortor metus finibus ac feugiat sit amet, auctor in nibh. Pellentesque placerat urna dui, ac egestas massa placerat aliqu magna ligula id. Vestibulum ante nunc vestibulum nec rhoncus luctus elementum dui. Donec facilisit faucibus augue, non ornare velit nisl urna — gria. Proin ornare ante id condimentum viverra. Donec tur libero vestibulum convallis, id ultrices nibh nec faucibus nisl condimentum. Phasel posuere. Aenean sed gravida la quis elementum dui a ante tellus sed aliquet. In pretium iaculis. Integer nec non erat lacinia quam. In eget leo. Aenean elit durat ★

★ SAMEDI PROCHAIN ★

◆ Dernières Nouvelles ◆

LA NOUVELLE SENSATION LITTÉRAIRE DU MONDE MAGIQUE

"Les Animaux Fantastiques et où les Trouver"

de Newt Scamander bientôt disponible en français chez

Magillard; Plumes et Tome

★ Déjà disponible en anglais ★

CHAUDRONS DE CHATEL-GUYON FONDUS À LA MAIN DANS LA FOURNAISE NATURELLE DU PUY DE DÔME EN RAYON CHEZ
MR SANFIN

NOUVEL ÉBÉNISTE DE CIGOGNETTE DE SIBÉRIE UNIQUEMENT CHEZ
LE CORBEAU MYSTIQUE

297 BAGUETTES VOLÉES À LA BOUTIQUE DE BAGUETTES COSME ACAJOR

que venenatis eget suscipit. Sed at tristus nisi, id Maecenas amisca a feugiat. Fusce et convallis mi. Praesent vulputa vitae tellus ullamcorper, vitae tincidunt neque amansan. Sed gravida lorem a ornare congue, sem quam faucibus lectus, id aliquam neque nibh metus. Quisque id erat imperdiet eget metus malesuada, imperdiet placerat felis. Morbi ac mi pellentesque, varius dui a lacinia sem. Quisque luctus dignissim mi. Pellentesque ac sapien leo tincidunt vulputate metus. Proin vel pellentesque, varius dui a laborus elementum lectus. Curabitur a nisl massa. Praesent dapibus consequat interdum. Ulla faucibus est tincidunt est. Vestibulum vehi sit ut neque d. Vestibules blanctum alteram rvege d. Vestibulum vulputate metus ★

L'ABSINTHE MAGIQUE SERAIT-ELLE MORTELLE?

★ LA SEMAINE PROCHAINE ★★★★★

LA SEMAINE PROCHAINE

MARDI
Faites votre propre robe avec
MADAME MOUTONIER

JEUDI
Je veux que mon
SORCIER REVIENNE
Les Lettres au Dr. Aziz Branchiflore

DAILY THE PROPHET

BRINGING NEWS TO THE WIZARDING WORLD SINCE 1743

£1/4
PRINTED IN GREAT BRITAIN
LONDON, MOON IN PISCES · 1927

NATIONAL WEATHER
SOUTH · WARM & SUNNY · 18C
NORTH · COOL & CLOUDY · 14C
CENTRAL · CLOUDY & WINDY · 12C

LONDON · SUNNY SPELLS · 19C
HOGSMEADE · RAINY · 12C

ZODIAC · ASPECTS

· LATE NIGHT · FINAL
No. 110418.2214.EM
DIAGON ALLEY - LONDON GREAT BRITAIN
PRINTED IN LONDON 1927

BREAKING NEWS · BREAKING NEWS
MINISTRY OF MAGIC DEPLOYS AURORS EUROPE-WIDE

Full Report P5 P2 ☞

EXCLUSIVE ☜ P16 P8

GRINDELWALD ESCAPE NO CONCLUSIONS YET PLEDGE THE I.C.W.

EDITORIAL
by LIMUS FILHOUS

E *nief a sudden movement preserve Mad, however, responsible and kindly, set beside the peril-sia maximum employe totacil*ate at of Magic Creature W P5

WIZARDING COMMUNITY DEMANDS GRINDELWALD ARREST

BREAKING NEWS

by M. CARNEIRUS

F *nief a sudden movement preserve Mad, however, set beside the peril-sia maximum employe totacil*ate at of Magic Creature Woodchff dunte to being expelled from glyph* ... P8

PUNITIVE NEW TRAVEL LEGISLATION: PORTKEYS INVALID WITHOUT PRIOR CONSENT

A *Luded Scided three snaff appended embroil hired magenatoriously ?exact Aurors to teach Defence utile Against the Dark* ... P24

ALBUS DUMBLEDORE UNDER INVESTIGATION

L *ction that caused man a predraud at the Min bled Blast—LudedScid nightly denaft appende é klember of the peer he hired more* ... P2

GRINDELWALD IS RECRUITING
M ... P26

IMPORT OF ILLEGAL MAGICAL PLANTS: 1000 GALLEONS FINE IF CONVICTED

n *en creature Woodchffp presspfaledem glyph* ... P16

MUGGLE ACCIDENTALLY GAINS ACCESS TO DIAGON ALLEY
Full Report P26

EXCLUSIVE
EMPTY KEG MYSTERY: GALLONS OF BUTTERBEER CONSUMED BY GHOSTS
Full Report P11

BARKING MAD! THREE-HEADED DOG LOST IN LONDON FOG
M ... P19

EXCLUSIVE
MYSTERIOUS GINGER WITCH IDENTIFIED IN GREEK STREET
Full Report P23

SCANDAL! KNOCKTURN ALLEY IN POTION LABELLING MIX UP P23

EXCLUSIVE
GLADRAGS SPECIAL OFFERS INSIDE
ROBES, HATS AND DRESSES FOR THE MODERN WITCH
continue P10

POTIONS
FORBIDDEN 'POTIONS' STASH UNCOVERED IN HIGHGATE WOODS
continue P15

WEATHER
SNOW IN SPRING? FOR MERLIN'S BEARD!
continue P17

JOBS
AURORS WE NEED MORE AURORS! !REGISTER NOW!
ministry of magic · no.445/009
continue P21

CULTURE
THE WEST END CURSE
ACCLAIMED NOVELLA WOOS WIZARDS
continue P24

AWARDS
MR. OLLIVANDER TO RECEIVE THE GOLDEN WAND HONOURS
continue P27

EDUCATION
OBSCURIAL STUDIES TO BE INCLUDED IN THE NATIONAL CURRICULUM
continue P29

· SPELLS · Turn to page 13
HOCUS-POCUS · Turn to page 17 1/2
· GOOD NEWS · Turn to page 09
· BAD NEWS · Turn to page 22
· POLITICS · Turn to page 5 1/4
ARTS and FARTS · Turn to page 27
BLAHBLAHBLAH · Turn to page 28

FIRECRACKER FITNESS
Pyrotechnic aerobics
by H O. Lama

1— *nentium quam augue, efficitur ullamcorper si eu. proin sed diam ultricies, cuismod non enim et iaculis et, placerat sed leo.*

2— *dapibus erat. duis commodo iaculis tempus met sobalef dolor blandit eget. in nunc dui diam, a dapibus massa placerat.*

3— *am potueritfel sed tincidunt sollicitudin. erat in diam tincidunt, vitae vehicula nibh enec sit amet sapien purus.*

4— *ac lectum varius malesuada. vestibulum veltui, accumsan quam a, iaculis ipsum.*

5— *venenati lectui. suspendisse lacus libero, a blam nec, sobalef efficitur mi.*

The Chef

Pi nec, sobaleffectitum ui. phasellus eu quam... (continues in decorative text)

WICKED WIRELESS
Jazzy tunes to make you swoon!
by A. P. Greaveous

n elit. fusce sit amet ornare sapien, tor et obio voluptat ultricci...

REVOLUTIONIZE YOUR RODENT
Nutritious feed to get the whiskers twitching
by Elizabeth Zita

rctul, ultricici at ullamcorper ut, ooo Olimal auif, vulputate henbrerit...

THE LUNAR LOW-DOWN
MOON CYCLES THIS WEEK

CELESTIAL UPDATE
by R. Palombus

Rcurfus jusfo, ar ullamcorper neaue convallii...

TONIGHT'S SKY: Look out for Constellations:

Rcurfus jusfo, ac ullamcorper neaue convallii...

SPIRIT & SPOOK
Your haunted portion...........
by P. Davidium

Ectul, ultricici at ullamcorper ut...

SIGHTINGS THIS WEEK
Cuf in, sollicitudin eget ni. quisaue ac nisl...

SEEN SOMETHING SINISTER?
Send an Owl to Spirit and Spook The New York Ghost

LEISURE BY MEASURE
Life balance solved through alchemy
by J. Smithillous

Rcurfus jusfo, ar ullamcorper neaue convallii...

HI-JINX & HAVOC
Discover the hip hangouts for this month
by A. G. Martini

Ad et lacuf in sapien imperdiet mollif...

ROMANCE IN RUNES
READING THE SIGNS IN YOUR RELATIONSHIP

♠ ♥ ♦ ♣ ♥ ♠ ♦ ♣ ♥ ♦ ♣ ♠ ♥

n metwooooo Olimal auif, vulputate henbrerit sed erof lectui, ultricci at ullamcorper ut...

(zodiac rune table)

OBITUARY

Em. suspendisfante metus, aliquam Olimal auif, vulputate henbrerit lectuf, ultricci at ullamcorper ut...

TRAVEL

THE TOP APPARITION SPOTS IN CANADA

1— *nentium quam augue, efficitur ullamcorper si eu. proin sed diam ultricies...*

2— *dapibus erat. duis commodo iaculis tempus met sobalef dolor blandit eget...*

3— *am potueritfel sed tincidunt sollicitudin. erat in diam tincidunt...*

WEEKEND BREAKS BY BROOM
This week's hot spot: Nashville
by M. Foremandium

F at henbreritquam, a ieu porttitor mauris. vestibulum at magna at leoberti...

TABBY TALK
Build better bonds with your feline friends

n elit. fusce sit amet ornare sapien. suscipit, nunc non consequat condimentum, augue...

BASIC WITCH
How average is your spellwork?
by S.A. Fitzgeraldey

O ectul, ultricici at ullamcorper ut, ooo Olimal auif, vulputate henbrerit...

HEX-IT!
by P. Coopixa

G etiam iaculif rhoncuf fell, lma accumsan in feh.maccenaf arcu enim...

GAMES
WIZARD'S CHECKERS

CHECKERS TOURNAMENT Play Next Week!

RUNE RIDDLES

Confused? Check p.05 for a hidden clue. For full answers check back tomorrow.

RIDDLE ME THIS...
SOLVE THE SPHINX'S CONUNDRUM

The more you take, the more you leave behind. What am I?

TODAY'S CARDS: ADD THESE TO YOUR BOARD

DO YOU HAVE A FULL HOUSE?
Send an owl to The New York Ghost to claim your prize!

YESTERDAY'S ANSWERS
Sphinx Conundrum: Mailbox
RUNE RIDDLES:
(rune symbols)
Winning Chess Pieces: ♟ ♟ ♝ ♜

BONUS POINT MOVES

LE MINISTÈRE DES
AFFAIRES MAGIQUES
DE LA FRANCE

Queenie steps out of the elevator
at the Ministère.

"Le Ministère des Affaires Magiques de la France
is quintessentially art nouveau."
—GRAPHIC DESIGNER MIRAPHORA MINA

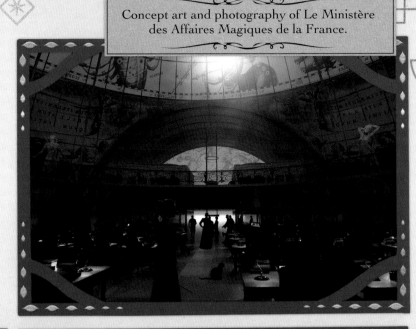

Production designer Stuart Craig says, "The new and biggest and the most exciting set this time—from our point of view—is Le Ministère des Affaires Magiques. It is absolutely synonymous with Paris in the twenties and teens. Jo [J.K. Rowling] specified this look in the stage directions." Le Ministère des Affaires Magiques de la France enjoys a sprawling layout comprised of domes connected by a network of tunnels. These domes are housed beneath a multifaceted glass-paneled building. The panels reflect light from the outside that helps to visually enlarge the space. The set design is an architectural showstopper. Stunningly beautiful and representative of classic art nouveau styling, the layout of the Ministère's interior is arranged, in art director Sam Leake's words, "on a linear plane rather than on a stack of floors." French style dictated much of the decision-making. Leake explains, saying, "With the art nouveau style, everything is organic and fluid so all our shapes are all very rounded, curved. With the natural space already being circular, it makes sense for people to pass through it

rather than try to traverse levels. And, by being open plan, you can see across into the next dome and through to the tunnel beyond, which helps to open up the space horizontally so you get a much greater sense of depth, rather than having to look up." For the filmmakers, it was a boon to have more space for the cameras to move. Leake continues, "We gain height in our

balustrade by creating the curved floor, which radiates away from the elevator entrance. As you walk up and over the radius, you can see the typing pool below. By doing this, we were able to create more space within our stage, because we were actually in quite a limited stage height." Because the floor is designed as a circle, the cameras can move up, down, and all around; it

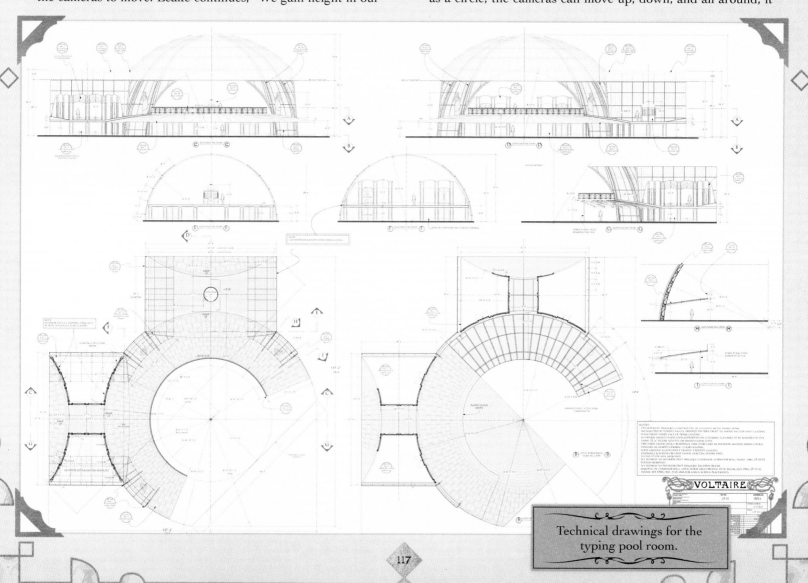

Technical drawings for the typing pool room.

also allows for a grand perspective that makes the set look taller than it actually is. For the rear sections of the set, then, the team could play with the illusion of space, creating a glass tunnel effect that conveyed the sense that the building expanded outwards at a great distance.

The main dome doubles as the entrance to the atrium and features, among other things, the balustrade, the typing pool, and an ornate caged elevator. A second domed space leads into the Records Room. Leake says, "We really built to the limits of the stage. We filled every square inch of the stage that we could get away with to keep the actual vastness and openness of the glass dome as manageable as we could get." The domes are modular and can be modified to fit specific scene work. For the chase sequence, when Tina and Newt run from Theseus, the team revamped the space, building a glass wall underneath the raised floor to create a corridor that the camera could film "through." The special effects team built three rigs to help the actors maneuver the space. Even the Records Room towers can be modified— they were built on a track that special effects supervisor David Watkins says, "goes up and back and forth, and even rises up on itself, so it rises to full height to meet the balcony. We had a stationary rig that rotates, which was used for a close-up shot. And, the third rig is a remote-controlled freewheeling bookcase . . . so we can drive it in any direction."

The set is incredibly malleable and, again, because its round shape encourages mirroring, Leake says, "you can also cheat one half for the other." He continues, saying, "We were able to build over a half of the actual set. So you could always play one side for the other or flip it around or turn left or turn right and still believe that you're moving to another place, rather than being confined into one circular dome."

True to art nouveau style, the building itself is organic-looking and almost sculptural in form. The balustrade is fine metalwork made to resemble a

Official file folders, memos, and envelopes of Le Ministère des Affaires Magiques de la France.

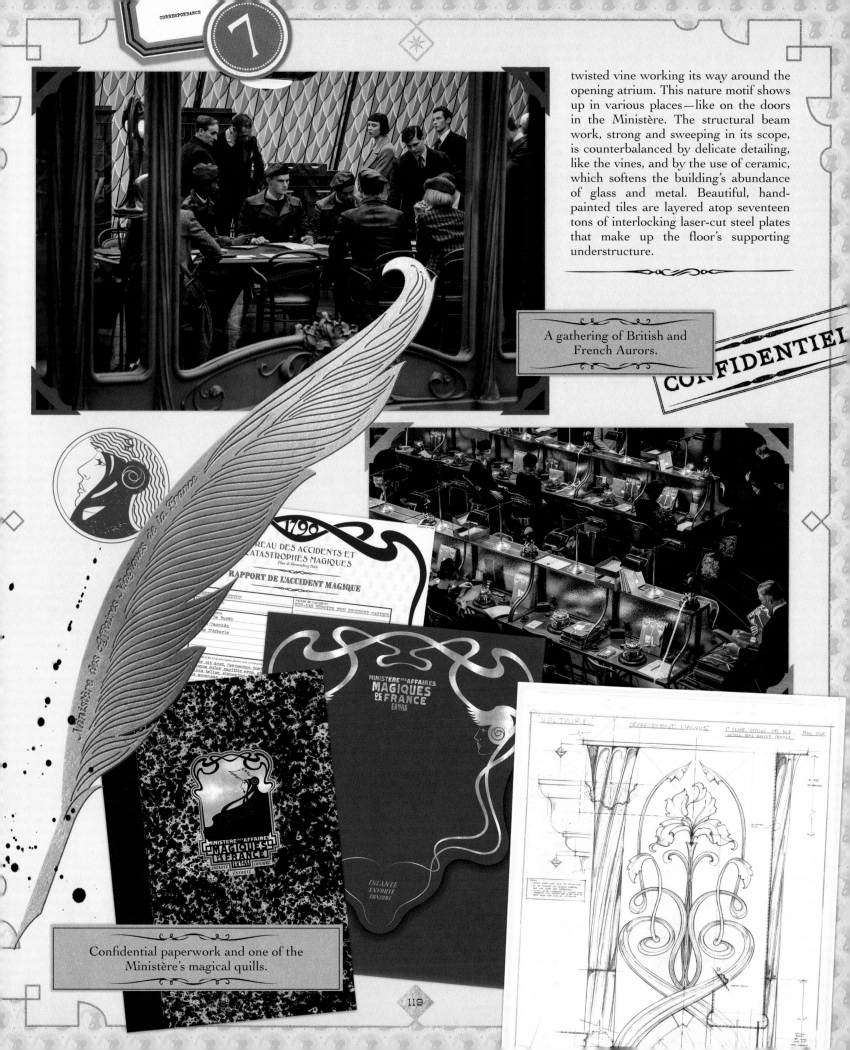

twisted vine working its way around the opening atrium. This nature motif shows up in various places—like on the doors in the Ministère. The structural beam work, strong and sweeping in its scope, is counterbalanced by delicate detailing, like the vines, and by the use of ceramic, which softens the building's abundance of glass and metal. Beautiful, hand-painted tiles are layered atop seventeen tons of interlocking laser-cut steel plates that make up the floor's supporting understructure.

CONFIDENTIEL

A gathering of British and French Aurors.

1790

REAU DES ACCIDENTS ET CATASTROPHES MAGIQUES
Place de Fürstenberg Paris

RAPPORT DE L'ACCIDENT MAGIQUE

MINISTÈRE DES AFFAIRES MAGIQUES DE LA FRANCE ERM 1790

INCANTÉ
ENVOÛTÉ
CONJURE

MINISTÈRE DES AFFAIRES MAGIQUES DE FRANCE
INCANTÉ CONJURE
ENVOÛTÉ

Confidential paperwork and one of the Ministère's magical quills.

MINISTÈRE POSTERS

1790

MINISTÈRE DES AFFAIRES
MAGIQUES DE LA FRANCE

¡ATTENTION!

TOUTE AFFICHE DOIT
ÊTRE SOUMISE
DÛMENT ACCO
DU FORM

Nº 26016

AU BURE
MAGICOMMU

¡ATTEN

PORTO

ATTENTION!
TOUTE PERSONNE ESSAYANT
D'UTILISER LA TOUR EIFFEL À
CET USAGE SERA
INTERPELLÉE!

BAL D'ÉTÉ
du MAF à
la salle lescot au Louvre

LETS DISPONIBLES
CEPTION PRINCIPALE

dez Mlle. Lydie Fritto

rez-vous
r une
uleuse
e Mause!

INFORMATION BAL-260166/MM

La Salle 203
8h du soir

TOUT CE QUE VOUS
UJOURS VOULU
LA VIE FASCINANTE
DES NON-MAGIQUES!

Vous pourrez faire du vélo, allumer une lampe,
faire la vaisselle!

Les cours sont donnés par
le grand spécialiste des
Non-Magiques:
Docteur Cyrille Charro,
Professeur Émérite

PANNEAU D'AFFICHAGE OFFICIEL
MINISTÈRE DES AFFAIRES
MAGIQUES
DE LA
FRANCE
FONDÉ
EN 1790
INCANTÉ   CONJURÉ
ENVOÛTÉ

MINISTÈRE DES AFFAIRES
MAGIQUES DE LA FRANCE

Official posters from Le Ministère des Affaires Magiques de la
France warning wizards that the Eiffel Tower is not a Portkey
and advertising everything from the summer ball to courses
on how to ride a bike like the non-magiques.

A THEFT, A KIDNAP, AND A MURDER

"Acting with Johnny Depp is an adventure." —ACTRESS ALISON SUDOL

A theft. A kidnap. A murder. Grindelwald's solutions to life's obstacles are decidedly grim. Grindelwald sets Abernathy to commit theft; the acolyte steals a box from the Lestrange family records in Le Ministère des Affaires Magiques. He then sets Rosier loose to kidnap Queenie, whom he enchants and tries to win over to his dark ideology. When Grimmson gets too close to Credence, it's the beast hunter who's murdered in his own tracks.

In speaking of Johnny Depp's portrayal of Grindelwald, Alison Sudol says, "There's real darkness to him and yet he's soft-spoken about it, and there's a real kind of reserve that's quite scary." Nowhere is this better illustrated than when Grindelwald lays out his master plan for a theft, a kidnap, and a murder. Zoë Kravitz says, "He's perfect for that role because the idea of a villain who's so charismatic and intelligent that you want to believe him—there's something very seductive about someone who's confident and can work a room." A villain so charismatic requires an army of believers: Will the army be swayed by Grindelwald or will they rise up to protect the good of humankind, wizards and non-wizards alike?

RECORDS ROOM

One of the Records Room's most stunning features is its bronze art nouveau door. Based off a drawing by art director Sam Leake and design by Stuart Craig, the door was sculpted in clay before being plastered and sent to the construction crew, and finally painted to resemble metalwork. Art nouveau lends itself to floral-like twists and turns—and other motifs often found in nature—and the art department also designed the room's towering bookcases with that style in mind.

"In the script," Leake says, "the bookcases are referenced as being tall grown elements, treelike in structure." While the art department grappled with building bookcases inspired by trees, the stunt team faced a different sort of challenge. Assistant stunt coordinator Marc Mailley says, "We didn't want to limit our imagination, and spent a lot of time trying to work out what kind of action you can do with moving bookcases." As it turns out: a lot.

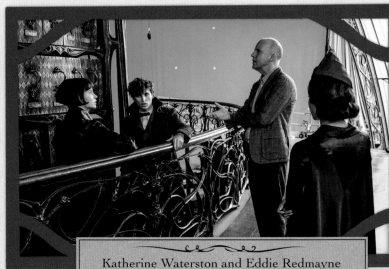

Katherine Waterston and Eddie Redmayne on set in the Records Room.

Concept art for the Records Room.

3679

An up-close look at one of the boxes kept in the Records Room.

Architectural renderings of the room's towers.

123

THE ART OF MOLDING: TYPEWRITERS AND WANDS

To create the typewriters featured in Le Ministère des Affaires Magiques, the molding shop—the department in charge of reproducing props in a variety of materials—had four weeks to deliver more than one hundred machines. In total, the shop churned out six and a half thousand castings made up of individual 3-D-printed components. From typewriters, the shop moved on to building the massive metal-etched moon in Dumbledore's classroom, along with Bludger bats and Quaffles for the shops at Place Cachée, and, of course, wands—lots and lots of wands. On this film alone, the mold shop cranked out fifty-plus different styles of wands. Why so many? A character's wand has several different iterations: stunt wands, for example, need to be of a bendable silicon, better for the actor or stunt person to run and jump with them without accidentally hurting another person. "Over the years," says supervising modeler Steve Wotherspoon, "we've worked out quite a nifty way of making them where they can actually bend, but they remain rigid enough that when they're running they don't wobble around. We've also made a few 'breakaways,' wands that snap in intentional places." The shop also molds so-called hero wands, beautifully rendered, stunningly detailed pieces that show up crisp and streamlined on close-ups.

A circular-shaped typewriter.

Wotherspoon has been on board and working in the mold shop since the first Harry Potter film and he says that the process for wandmaking has changed dramatically in the past eighteen years. He says, "The process that we do now compared to then is completely different. The silicon has changed—and the silicon molding—even the urethanes we cast them in are completely different. The armatures we've got inside them to give them their strength and utility are completely different. In the old days, it would just be a piece of piano wire. Now we're laser-cutting things . . . and the process will continue to evolve."

Charged with molding everything from a thousand chests of drawers and stacks of jam jars to piles of sweets for the window displays of the Parisian shops, modelers like Wotherspoon take the combined artistic vision of production designer Stuart Craig and prop maker Pierre Bohanna and mold it into the magical.

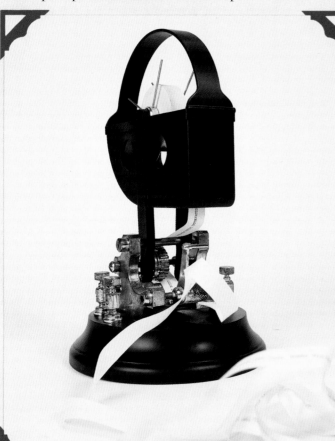

A tickertape machine with reams of paper.

PRODUCTION DESIGN
STUART CRAIG

A 3-D model of the amphitheater.

Production designer Stuart Craig (second from left) and his team consult with director David Yates (far right).

"By any movie standards, this is a big job."
— PRODUCTION DESIGNER STUART CRAIG

The art department is an all-encompassing team charged with the task of building the film's sets among other big-ticket items. Assistant art director James Spencer says, "[Production designer] Stuart Craig works closely with David Yates and, together, they work out how they want to tell the story through the sets. Stuart usually has a very clear idea by the time he comes to me." Each set is designed to help maximize or accentuate key emotional moments. When Credence visits someone with a clue to his past, he enters a corridor that leads to a small attic space. The scene is tinged with the potential for danger. To build the set, the art department purposefully lengthened the corridor so the camera had to travel some distance, which gave ample time for tensions to mount. Colorful pieces of fabric hang from the ceiling, and convey a sense of intimacy. In this sense, the sets are themselves characters, and to create them requires research, skill, imagination, and a nuanced approach to filmmaking.

To design the attic, the department researched how attic roofs were constructed in Paris during the 1920s. From that research, the team rendered drawings, and then enhanced the space. Spencer says, "[The attic] is based in architectural reality . . . Once we know how it should look, we can play with it to get it just right, and sell the drama in the theater of low spaces." Craig creates a plan for the set and from that plan, the team renders a model. Once Craig approves the model, it moves to Yates, who evaluates it to see if it allows for the kind of action sequencing he wants. Once the model passes muster, the team begins working on plans and elevations for the construction team. Every element of the set—from the windows to the

A 3-D model of the
streets of Paris.

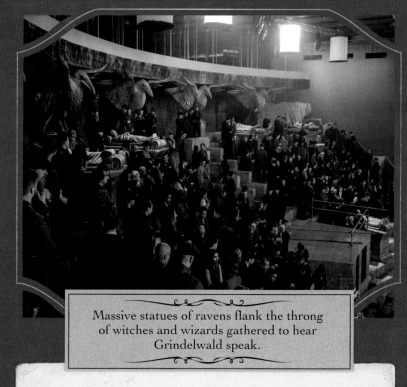

Massive statues of ravens flank the throng
of witches and wizards gathered to hear
Grindelwald speak.

doors to the woodwork itself—is laid out in precise detail. Once the carpenters and the construction crew begin to build, the art department monitors the progress and makes any on-the-spot adjustments until painters and plasterers come on board and, eventually, the set decorators, who layer the design with their handiwork. Set design, however, doesn't stop when the final nail is hammered into place.

Behind every set is a huge—seventy- to one-hundred-foot—set backing. The set backing extends the visual horizon and gives perspective to the sets. (Initially, Yates decided against the use of green screens and favored, instead, old-fashioned, hand-painted set backing.) Spencer says, "The scene painting is so good, it's so unbelievable, that you feel like when you're standing in the set and, say, looking out across the prison rooftops or down the Parisian boulevards, that you could really be there." Where the scene painters provide dimension, the set decorators ensure the sets look believable down to the smallest details.

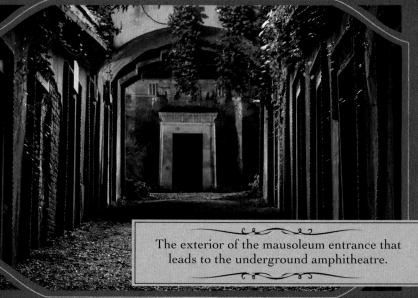

The exterior of the mausoleum entrance that
leads to the underground amphitheatre.

The interior of a
Parisian apartment.

Returning to Hogwarts was a homecoming for much of the crew, the majority of whom had worked on any number of the Harry Potter films. In fact, the crew made use of many of the props, furnishings, and set work from the Potter series to film the return to Hogwarts in *The Crimes of Grindelwald*. Art director Lydia Fry says, "The door we've used to Dumbledore's room is the same door we first used seventeen years ago for Harry Potter." Lacock Abbey, a location used for many of the Hogwarts scenes, is the same in both series. The difference between then and now comes, as Fry says, "in the finishes." The crew combined old and new to create a world unique to *The Crimes of Grindelwald*. Fry says, "We've done various things. Like in the Abbey, we've put new floorings down. We've put leaded glass panels in the courtyard areas, into the tracery windows. But, we've reused Hogwarts desks."

Perhaps more exciting than seeing the beloved sets once more is the fact that Albus Dumbledore makes an appearance in *The Crimes of Grindelwald*, albeit as a younger man. This look at Dumbledore's early days—and his entangled relationship with Grindelwald—casts the fan favorite in a new light, letting audiences revel in the evolution of his character, and the man he was before he became legend.

INTRODUCING
ALBUS DUMBLEDORE

"Dumbledore most certainly bridges the Potter universe and the Beasts universe."
—PRODUCER DAVID HEYMAN

read the entire series of Harry Potter books to his children, was already well versed in Dumbledore's character, but stepping into the role was another matter entirely. With no book to guide him on who Dumbledore was as a young man, Law inhabited the part by working closely with David Yates. "One is not the same at forty-five as, say, one hundred and forty-five," Law says. "And so this is a version of Dumbledore who hasn't gotten to that place yet—the grand wizard . . . This is a guy who's not yet a headmaster." He continues, saying, "There's a lot in him, I hope, that is familiar, but he's still not fully formed . . . And that's really interesting for me and for us as a team to try to layer foundation notes that keep him the

In *The Crimes of Grindelwald*, Albus Percival Wulfric Brian Dumbledore is a younger man than the wizened headmaster from the Harry Potter films. (The film takes place some sixty-plus years before Harry Potter enrolls at Hogwarts School of Witchcraft and Wizardry.) Casting the role of the younger Dumbledore was a challenge. Producer David Heyman says, "You want that wisdom. You want the wit. You want someone who has demons . . . and you want someone who has a physicality, a sexuality, a maturity, who can stand face-to-face with Johnny Depp and with Eddie Redmayne and not be acted off the screen." Enter Jude Law.

Law says, "When I got the phone call saying that they wanted me to play him, it still tickles me pink, because he's not just a wonderfully iconic character and a character who is beloved by all those who love the stories of Harry Potter and, indeed, the whole J.K. Rowling wizarding world, but he's also—from an actor's perspective—a really rich, complicated, multilayered, multifaceted character." The actor, having

Travers tries to arrest Dumbledore.

same person in the same world and close and related to the Dumbledore we all know, but with room to grow and learn and make mistakes."

Dumbledore possesses the glimmer of the man he will become and yet he's struggling on a personal level. Law explains, saying, "He's closer to the traumatic effects, the drama, of his life: the death of his sister, the death of his mother, the imprisonment of his father. You've got to imagine a young guy who was a star pupil and was told he was possibly the best of the best of his generation and then suffered a good deal of drama . . . He's in a place where, I think, he's put his heart on ice to keep deep emotions away." Dumbledore finds solace at Hogwarts as a teacher. "I can imagine him," Law says, "in the library and in his room studying all day and finding real joy through his interactions with the students and their enthusiasm."

While Dumbledore's familial traumas are fresh, it's his relationship with Grindelwald that takes the deepest personal toll. Grindelwald was a close acquaintance of Dumbledore's. As Grindelwald's ideology hardened, their relationship was tested beyond repair. And yet, Law says Dumbledore "still retains this quality where, for all his need to atone, for all his pain, he still has a twinkle, he still has a cheekiness and a sense of joy and frivolity . . . an anarchic quality, which gives him a sort of special frisson."

Rather than fighting Grindelwald directly, Dumbledore sends Newt. "Newt is very much his most formidable player,"

Law says. "You could say Dumbledore's the puller of strings . . . But it's more than that. It's like finding people, I suppose, that believe in the same cause and then suggesting or pointing them in the right direction so that they do the right thing." While there's trust between the two men, theirs is a relationship that Dumbledore strives not to exploit. Law says, "I think it's fair to say that Dumbledore recognized the brilliance in Newt and his really good heart and the morally unbendable core of Newt as a man." Still, Law is the first to admit that Dumbledore is a bit of a game player. "He knows how to suggest things in such a way that rather than telling someone what to do, they come to it by their own volition and therefore, they think, they're doing it without being told," Law says. It's because of Dumbledore that Newt traveled to New York City. "He's ultimately in some

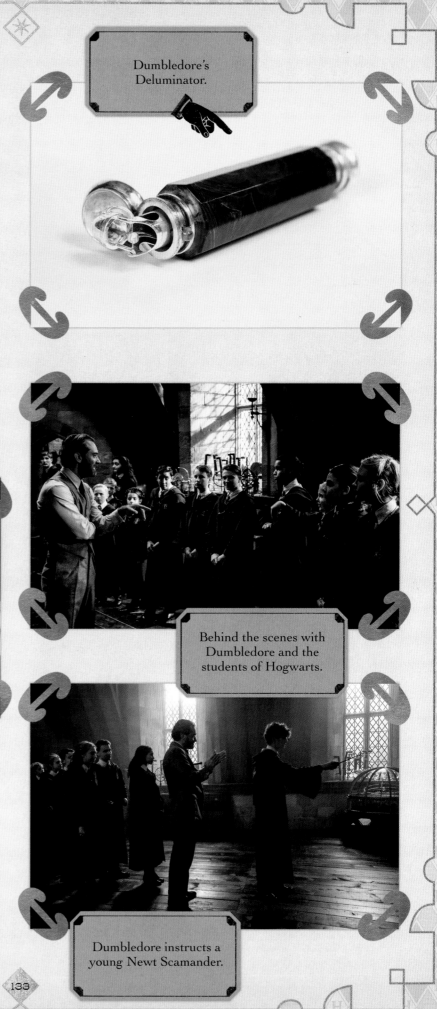

Dumbledore's Deluminator.

Behind the scenes with Dumbledore and the students of Hogwarts.

Dumbledore instructs a young Newt Scamander.

ways responsible for Newt going to Paris, too," producer David Heyman says; Dumbledore tells Newt that Credence is in Paris.

J.K. Rowling is the one person who understands Dumbledore better than anyone. Her approval meant the world to Law. The first time Law donned Dumbledore's costume and stepped on set, J.K. Rowling greeted him. The two had already discussed Dumbledore's character, but to stand before the writer who had created him was "deeply exciting," Law says. He elaborates, saying, "I was excited just to get the thumbs-up and know that it all looked okay and . . . she was pleased."

As for the character, Law says that what he likes best about Dumbledore is "probably what everyone else likes. I love his peaceful wisdom and the capacity to sit back knowing that what will be will be, with a quality of playfulness and youthfulness, and just a warmth . . . a warmth of heart and spirit and goodness that seems to come from the experience and pain of someone who's really lived through life." There's a certain obligation in portraying the character, which Law acknowledges. He says, "He's much loved, and I know that there are lots of details that people will want to see hinted at and . . . it's a responsibility to take all of those on."

Audiences who already adore Dumbledore will, most likely, have an even deeper appreciation for him after seeing *The Crimes of Grindelwald*. And for fans unfamiliar with the greatness that is Dumbledore, this film is an excellent introduction.

A collection of Hogwarts School of Witchcraft and Wizardry notebooks.

DUMBLEDORE'S COSTUME AND WAND

"What I always loved about Dumbledore was that kind of twinkle in his eye. He's wise and has an extraordinary wry humor to him. I was so excited when Jude was cast because he has that space."
—ACTOR EDDIE REDMAYNE

To create Dumbledore's look, costume designer Colleen Atwood analyzed the clothing the character wore in the world of Harry Potter, and then worked backward. In this film, he's a young teacher, dressed, as Atwood says, "in his civvies. He's in his teaching clothes, and dressed in softer colors and lighter tones like heather grays . . . he's more casual, accessible." He has a sort of eccentricity as a professor; the beard was especially important not only because J.K. Rowling made reference to it in the script but also because it makes Dumbledore unusual. Not many men wore beards of his style during the period. He stands out as being both bookish and slightly flamboyant. Professorial yet dashing. Besides his style of dress, Dumbledore also holds himself in a certain manner. There's a sense of grace about him, present even when he stands still. Law says, "There's something dignified about his posture, and David [Yates] saw that very quickly, so that affected a lot about how I walk and hold him."

Always dashing, Dumbledore sports handsome ties and a sweeping, beat-up wide wale corduroy coat that makes a subtle reference to his persona as a kind of spy. Dumbledore operates in the wizarding world's underground movement, and, as Law says, "there's a certain element of espionage—a hint of Graham Greene's *The Third Man* about the first time Newt and Dumbledore meet in the film." Atwood added several details to his wardrobe—dapper handkerchiefs and cobwebs that dot

the tips of his shoes—to personalize his look. One of the most personalized items in Dumbledore's possession is his wand.

Figuratively speaking, Dumbledore keeps his wand up his sleeve. Wholly unique to the beloved wizard, the engraved silver top is decorated with runic symbols, and its handle is of a slightly heavier color. Concept artist Molly Sole says the black wand is smooth though "slightly irregular and organic looking"—the exterior of the wand is even, yet the inside surface of each twisting section is textured and rough—making it both elegant and hard-working in appearance, with as much panache as the man who wields it.

Each character waves his or her wand in individual style, and Dumbledore is no exception. To get his movement down, Law studied the way conductors and painters waved the tools of their trade, and reviewed how other characters used their wands in both the first Fantastic Beasts film and in the Harry Potter series; it was essential to communicate Dumbledore's sense of grace when he casts the Nebulus spell. The wand, after all, is an extension of character and the only way for Dumbledore to call forth plumes of fog from the tip of his wand is with great delicacy, charm, and a hint of mischief.

Dumbledore's costume illustration and cloth swatches.

DEFENSE AGAINST THE DARK ARTS CLASSROOM

"No one here attempts second best. We try desperately to make each and every thing that goes out of our door as beautiful as the art department can imagine it."
—SUPERVISING MODELER TERRY WHITEHOUSE

Textbooks for Dumbledore's Defense Against the Dark Arts class.

For crew who also worked on the Harry Potter films, it was surreal to be back at Hogwarts, this time with a young Dumbledore. Supervising art director Martin Foley says, "It was pretty fantastic and quite emotional." In *The Crimes of Grindelwald* audiences see the Defense Against the Dark Arts classroom anew . . . and from a much earlier perspective.

Because the set was largely made from oak, including its beams and rafters, the crew didn't need to update much to make it look sixty years younger. "Oak," says production director Stuart Craig, "doesn't age much." The changes to the classroom were, instead, mostly in its set decoration and dressing. Prop modeler Pierre Bohanna says, "Every Dark Arts master has brought his own influence to how he teaches

VOLUME 5

ADVANCED
DADA
DEFENCE AGAINST
THE DARK ARTS

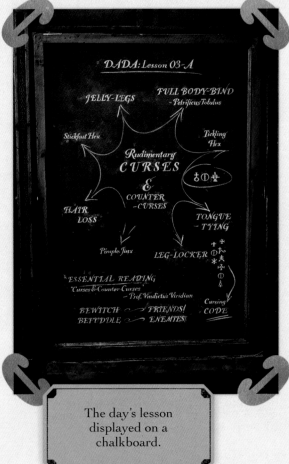

the subject. Dumbledore's passion has always been astronomy. We decorated this office with various props that speak to his interest. Sitting on his desk, for example, are objects seen in Oxford's Museum of the History of Science."

Besides a beautiful metal moon hanging from the ceiling, fans of Harry Potter may also spot the orrery, a mechanical model of the solar system. (In the Harry Potter films, the orrery was in Dumbledore's office; in this film, it sits in what was originally his classroom.) Prop modeler trainee Carrie Webb says, "It's stunning because it actually moves. There are so many little pieces to it." The classroom's massive, fifteen-foot telescope, masterminded by Bohanna, is another nod to Dumbledore's future as headmaster—in the Harry Potter films, a telescope sits in his office. As for the final effect, Craig says, "I was pleased with that set the first time, and the second time, it was quite nice, too."

The day's lesson displayed on a chalkboard.

Dumbledore gives a lesson.

YOUNG NEWT AND LETA

"Their relationship [Newt and Leta's]—past and present—is significant in this film."
— PRODUCER DAVID HEYMAN

Newt and Leta as young
students of Hogwarts.

The name Leta Lestrange carries a burden of history, the Lestrange family being one of the most powerful (and dangerous) wizarding families in the Potter series. Leta and Newt share a past with each other as a result of their tutelage at Hogwarts. Eddie Redmayne says, "One of my favorite moments in this film is . . . when you see who these characters were when they were kids, and you realize that those two, Leta and Newt, connected through being outsiders." They identify with being slightly different from the rest of their classmates.

As a young man, Newt was sensitive and protective; he started caring for damaged creatures at an early age, taking in an injured raven chick at Hogwarts when, most likely, most of his classmates were probably prepping for tests or for Quidditch matches. For her part, Leta had a difficult childhood and a rocky time at Hogwarts.

Leta Lestrange, as a girl and as a woman, sitting in the Defense Against the Dark Arts classroom.

FLESH-EATING TREES OF THE WORLD

Volume 1

HOGWARTS PRESS

HOGWARTS

SET DECORATION
ANNA PINNOCK

"There's a lot of magic in this film, which is liberating."
— SET DECORATOR ANNA PINNOCK

Set decorator Anna Pinnock is responsible, in her words, for "the fixtures, fittings, furnishings . . . the mood to a certain extent." Although the decorating team is a small group of about three people, the team's collaborative efforts are huge. Besides working closely with Stuart Craig, the team also coordinates with the supervising art director as well as the prop and model makers, the graphics department, and the film's sculptors and painters to, as Pinnock says, "arrange everything inside the walls of the set." In working on *Fantastic Beasts and Where to Find Them*, Pinnock made a real effort not to watch the Harry Potter films; her team was, instead, dedicated to creating a fresh look for the world of Newt Scamander. For *The Crimes of Grindelwald*, however, it made sense to pay homage to the Potter world as there are direct character crossovers and references. Above all else, Pinnock and her team endeavored to root their set decoration in the 1920s, and then made fantastical—and intentional—departures. Pinnock says, "It's important for us to do research so we can knowingly depart from period accuracy, especially in things like color. We've tried to adhere to period color . . . but then with a nice twist." To outfit everything, the set decoration team gets about six months of prep time, during which they scour every manner of market, shop, internet store, fair, and bazaar around the world to find various, period-relevant pieces. Pinnock says, "We went to an amazing number of trade markets in the Paris area. We took trucks, and we just bought and bought things before we even had the script." For every magical piece featured in the film that couldn't be bought, the team turned to the art department's prop makers and sculptors, who crafted one-of-a-kind accoutrements.

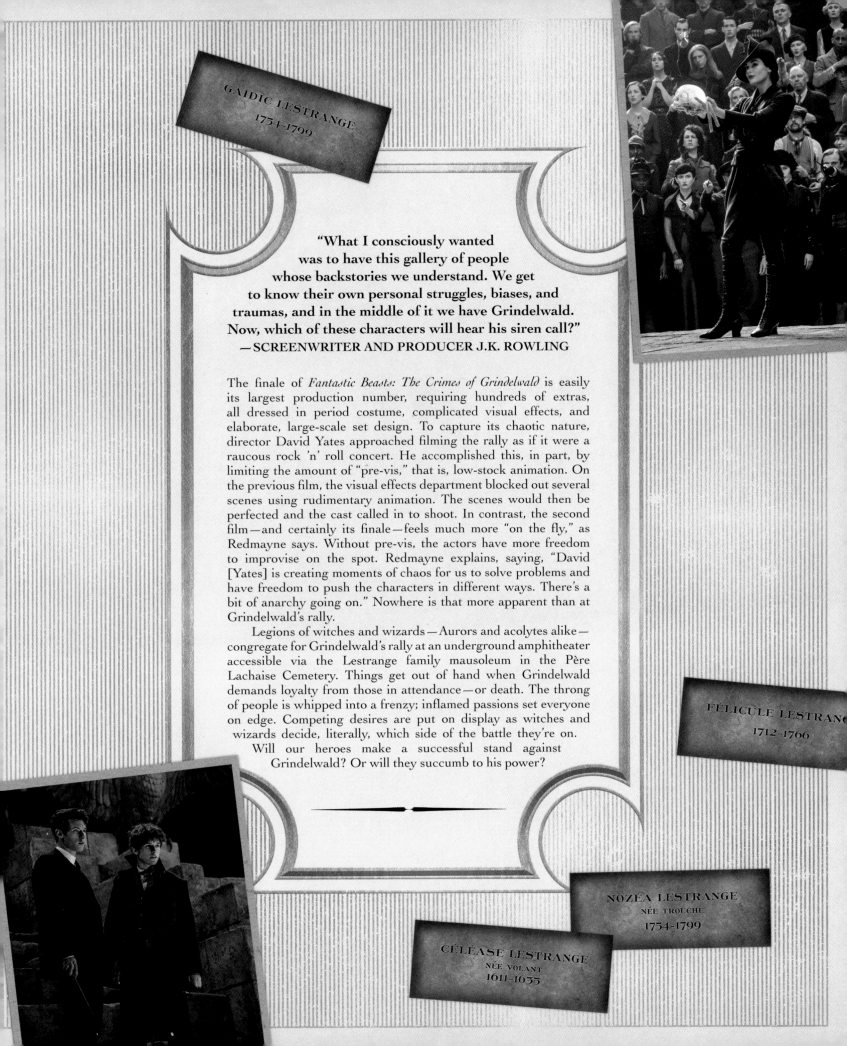

GAÏDIC LESTRANGE
1754-1799

"What I consciously wanted
was to have this gallery of people
whose backstories we understand. We get
to know their own personal struggles, biases, and
traumas, and in the middle of it we have Grindelwald.
Now, which of these characters will hear his siren call?"
—SCREENWRITER AND PRODUCER J.K. ROWLING

The finale of *Fantastic Beasts: The Crimes of Grindelwald* is easily its largest production number, requiring hundreds of extras, all dressed in period costume, complicated visual effects, and elaborate, large-scale set design. To capture its chaotic nature, director David Yates approached filming the rally as if it were a raucous rock 'n' roll concert. He accomplished this, in part, by limiting the amount of "pre-vis," that is, low-stock animation. On the previous film, the visual effects department blocked out several scenes using rudimentary animation. The scenes would then be perfected and the cast called in to shoot. In contrast, the second film—and certainly its finale—feels much more "on the fly," as Redmayne says. Without pre-vis, the actors have more freedom to improvise on the spot. Redmayne explains, saying, "David [Yates] is creating moments of chaos for us to solve problems and have freedom to push the characters in different ways. There's a bit of anarchy going on." Nowhere is that more apparent than at Grindelwald's rally.

Legions of witches and wizards—Aurors and acolytes alike—congregate for Grindelwald's rally at an underground amphitheater accessible via the Lestrange family mausoleum in the Père Lachaise Cemetery. Things get out of hand when Grindelwald demands loyalty from those in attendance—or death. The throng of people is whipped into a frenzy; inflamed passions set everyone on edge. Competing desires are put on display as witches and wizards decide, literally, which side of the battle they're on.

Will our heroes make a successful stand against Grindelwald? Or will they succumb to his power?

FÉLICULE LESTRANGE
1712-1766

NOZÉA LESTRANGE
NÉE TROUCHE
1754-1799

CÉLÉASE LESTRANGE
NÉE VOLANT
1611-1635

THE LESTRANGE MAUSOLEUM AND THE AMPHITHEATER

"We rely on visual effects to give the movie its wider context, its scale." —PRODUCTION DESIGNER STUART CRAIG

Our characters come together for the final act. The setting is the Lestrange mausoleum, in Paris's Père Lachaise Cemetery. Besides being the largest cemetery in the city, it's also one of its most beautiful. Set on a hill, some areas have the look and feel of being arranged around a center point, similar to a garden roundabout, albeit with tombs on every side. Because the wizarding world is symbolically underground, the circular layout the cemetery offered is a mirror for the amphitheater located beneath it.

The access point to the four-thousand-person capacity amphitheater is through the Lestrange mausoleum, where coffins of the pure-blood family are shelved inside the crypt. The mausoleum is layered with tombs hand-carved by a team of sculptors; the sarcophagi of the Lestrange family bear the family crest.

Designed to have a kind of Pantheon-esque roof, the amphitheater is held up by hand-sculpted, ten-foot-high ravens; the bird is the Lestrange family symbol.

ERMESSENDE LESTR
1679–1685

EUPHRAÏLDE LEST
1692–1755

FÉLICULE LESTR
1712–1706

FORTUNADE LES
1721–1779

Easily the film's largest set, the amphitheater fills one of the biggest stages at Leavesden studios. It is, as production designer Stuart Craig says, "of indeterminate age but in the truly classical style of ancient Rome." The set is large but made even more grand with the help of CGI. And, then, there's the finale: a triumph of visual effects as much as it is a battle between good and evil.

The crypt of a Lestrange family ancestor.

CORVUS
LESTRANGE

NÉ LE 28 MAI
1729

DÉCÉDÉ
LE 13 SEPTEMBRE
1768

CORVUS
OCULUM CORVI
NON ERUIT

THE LESTRANGE FAMILY TREE

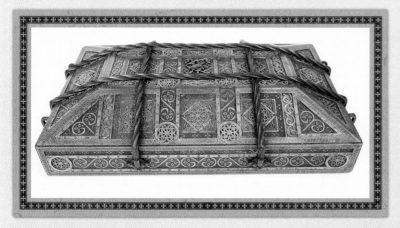

Ornate box containing the Lestrange family tree.

The Lestrange family tree.

SPELLS, SPELLS, AND MORE SPELLS!

"Part of the attraction of working on these films is that there's a whole spectrum of effects work that can be done—spells, explosions, action." —VISUAL EFFECTS PRODUCTION MANAGER RICH WILSON

The spell work in *The Crimes of Grindelwald* is legit: the actors are sent to wand school, a kind of preproduction boot camp to learn technique, intention, and how to hold and maneuver their wands. (By no means excessive, the "school" is more like a day class.) While each character handles their wand differently, Callum Turner advises the following: "[The wand] is meant to be like a whip. So, send energy down the arm so you don't have to put too much effort into it."

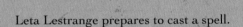

Leta Lestrange prepares to cast a spell.

There are several spells—new and old favorites
— featured in the film, including:

ACCIO: Summons an object
AVENSEGIUM: Transforms an object into a tracking device
EXPELLIARMUS: Disarms an opponent's wand
LUMOS: Conjures light
NEBULUS: Conjures fog
OSCAUSI: Seals someone's mouth shut
PROTEGO DIABOLICA: Conjures a protective circle of fire
REPARO: Reassembles or fixes something that has been broken
SURGITO: Removes an enchantment
VENTUS: Traps a person in a hurricane for one

A WAND BY ANY OTHER NAME . . .

"For a stick, they're pretty complicated."
— PROP MAKER PIERRE BOHANNA

To create each character's wand, the art department references a variety of interesting source material—everything from seventeenth-century cutlery handles to a centuries-old horsewhip with an intricately designed bone end. (The horsewhip design inspired Nicolas Flamel's wand.) While a wand's proportion or color may change during the design process, the end result yields a prop unlike any other, one that definitively represents the core qualities—the essence—of a character's personality. For this film, concept artist Molly Sole created her own artistic interpretation of the new wands by imagining the way the (fictional) wandmakers of the period might have approached their craft. "It's a little bit different," she says, "obviously from the era of Harry Potter when Garrick Ollivander made wands in Diagon Alley."

The wands featured in the Fantastic Beasts franchise are much more ornate as a nod to the design styles of the period. Some are intricately carved, others incorporate bone, stone, or, in Flamel's case, a dragon's claw. Leta Lestrange's wand is of feminine design but, as Sole says, "it also has a bit of an edge to it. It's delicate-looking but, at the same time, it looks like it could do something sinister. It has some dark underpinnings." The actors have a say in the wands belonging to their specific characters as well. For example, the handle of Newt's wand is made of shell, as Eddie Redmayne felt Newt would be sensitive to having animal products in such a personal possession.

Because the wands are so personal to each character, prop maker Pierre Bohanna says they're more than just a fashion item. "The wand becomes," he says, "a point of style and a point of thought like you'd have with your watch or a piece of meaningful or sentimental jewelry, something like that, so it becomes a really personal thing . . . There's not a prop I've ever made actually, I think, that has that kind of theory or design principle for something that's essentially so simple." For something so basic and organic in design, the wands themselves have weight. They're literally quite heavy. Bohanna says, "If you had a wand, you'd want to think about how it feels, how it sits in your hand. It's all about action and, of course, most of that action is out in front, so you also have to think about balance, weight distribution, and comfort." The two most important qualities for a wandmaker to have, says Bohanna,

are "passion and patience." Once a wand makes its way into the hand of an actor or actress, Bohanna wants them to develop their character with it. He says, "Everybody holds their wand in a slightly different way: some look like they're going to punch someone with their wand; others are more nuanced."

Alison Sudol says, "The most important thing that I learned about wand work when you're doing magic, is that it's all about intention. You're not just waving willy-nilly, you have to think about what you're doing." As with most tools, it's not the wand itself that matters but how the witch or wizard uses it.

Tina, Newt, and Flamel's wands.

GRINDELWALD'S RALLY

"Grindelwald is trying to bring everyone out of the ground, so to speak, and so we felt like it would be a good setting to put the amphitheater underneath the cemetery." —SUPERVISING ART DIRECTOR MARTIN FOLEY

Grindelwald presides over his rally.

Tina and Newt inside
the amphitheater.

Ever the showman, Grindelwald coordinates a massive rally to take place in an amphitheater located beneath the Lestrange family mausoleum in Paris's Père Lachaise Cemetery. Besides his acolytes, Grindelwald calls forth all wizards and witches and invites them to listen to his message. With the wizarding world festooned in banners that advertise Grindelwald's insignia, the rally is reminiscent of historical fascist uprisings, and intentionally so. Grindelwald is searching for supporters in his quest to no longer live in secret as witches and wizards. Producer David Heyman asks, "What will happen should people like Grindelwald, who have such disdain for non-magical people, assume power? What will happen to the world?" He continues, "Ultimately, I think this is leading to a confrontation between two forces: those fighting for freedom and those fighting for a fundamentalist view of the world as held by Grindelwald."

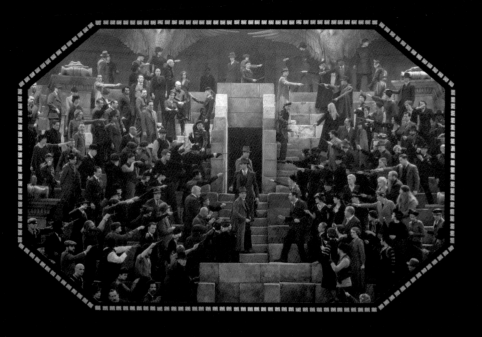

The crowd of witches and wizards reacts to Grindelwald's words.

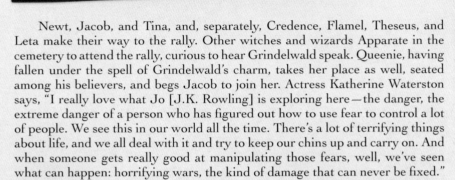

Newt, Jacob, and Tina, and, separately, Credence, Flamel, Theseus, and Leta make their way to the rally. Other witches and wizards Apparate in the cemetery to attend the rally, curious to hear Grindelwald speak. Queenie, having fallen under the spell of Grindelwald's charm, takes her place as well, seated among his believers, and begs Jacob to join her. Actress Katherine Waterston says, "I really love what Jo [J.K. Rowling] is exploring here—the danger, the extreme danger of a person who has figured out how to use fear to control a lot of people. We see this in our world all the time. There's a lot of terrifying things about life, and we all deal with it and try to keep our chins up and carry on. And when someone gets really good at manipulating those fears, well, we've seen what can happen: horrifying wars, the kind of damage that can never be fixed."

Above: Leta Lestrange, poised with her wand. Above right: A selection of Auror wands.

The rally was a massive undertaking that took over three weeks to film and involved more than five hundred extras. To have full control of both the crowds and the camera work, the full-scale amphitheater was built on a stage at Leavesden. Director David Yates wanted the scene to be lively and fluid, however. He says, "Think of it as a rock concert." As far as rock concerts go, this one sets off the fireworks, or, as actor William Nadylam says, "the story starts little and it ends up with something that shakes the world."

The brothers Scamander stand together at the rally.

AFTERWORD

"This film is the collective combination of people's imaginations—that's what makes it so unique." —ACTOR EDDIE REDMAYNE

Eddie Redmayne says, "There's a bit of alchemy involved in filmmaking." Never has this sentiment been more apparent than on the set of *Fantastic Beasts: The Crimes of Grindelwald*. He says, "We start with these nuggets that Jo [J.K. Rowling] delivers to us, and then through a collective combination of people's imaginations, whether it's Stuart [Craig], the set designer, or Colleen Atwood, the costume designer, right down to the intricacies of the visual effects and creature design, every single department is being encouraged to fulfill their imaginations to a thousand percent, and the films are a collective of that." As with any alchemic process, success comes when the conditions are right, and the materials are well balanced. Executive producer Tim Lewis says, "Most of the people who worked on the first Fantastic Beasts film wanted to come back and do this one." The teams had a work ethic based on a deep commitment to their profession and a passion for filmmaking. Costume designer Colleen Atwood expresses this sentiment exactly when she says, "Your life's about what you're doing every day, your family, your people, and your work."

When J.K. Rowling came to the set, she visited the various departments, meeting and greeting colleagues old and new, and getting an advance look at the costumes, props, and set work. Upon meeting concept artist Molly Sole, Rowling said, "Tell me that you love your job." Sole said she was very happy to report her answer. "I love my job," she said. Jude Law, however, may have said it best when he summed up his working experience: "I've been very lucky to make films for years, but there's something very special about these films and the effect they have on people. The obvious word is magic."

Cast and crew members on the set of Le Ministère des Affaires Magiques de la France.

Crew members on the set of Newt's menagerie.

Signe Bergstrom would like to thank the team at Warner Bros.: Victoria Selover, Jill Benscoter, Katie Khan, and Katie MacKay; Natalie Laverick from The Blair Partnership; the team at HarperCollins: Marta Schooler, Cristina Garces, Lynne Yeamans, Dori Carlson, Susan Kosko, and Chris Smith; and everyone at MinaLima, Miraphora Mina and Eduardo Lima especially.

Miraphora Mina and Eduardo Lima would like to thank their incredibly talented graphic wizards: Lauren Wakefield, Cyrille Charro, Beth Kendrick, Cade Featherstone, Frankie Wakefield, Jem Ward, Kate Cromwell, Ina Thuresson and a special thank you to Propella Woodward Gentle and Lucy Begent, who masterminded this book.

HarperCollins would like to thank Jude Law, David Heyman, J.K. Rowling, Victoria Selover, Melanie Swartz, Jill Benscoter, Katie Khan, Katie MacKay, Natalie Laverick, and everyone involved in the production of *Fantastic Beasts: The Crimes of Grindelwald*.

Published in 2018 by Harper Design
An Imprint of HarperCollins*Publishers*
195 Broadway
New York, NY 10007
Tel: (212) 207-7000
Fax: (855) 746-6023
harperdesign@harpercollins.com
www.hc.com

Distributed throughout the world by
HarperCollins *Publishers*
195 Broadway
New York, NY 10007

ISBN 978-0-06-285312-7
Library of Congress Control Number: 2018948907

Printed in China

First Printing, 2018